CHAOS POINT

2012 AND BEYOND

Also by Ervin Laszlo

Macroshift (Berret-Koehler, 2001)

You Can Change the World (Select Books, 2003)

The Connectivity Hypothesis (SUNY Press, 2003)

Science and the Akashic Field (Inner Traditions, 2004)

Science and the Reenchantment of the Cosmos (Inner Traditions, 2006)

The Akashic Experience (Inner Traditions, 2006)

WorldShift 2012 (Inner Traditions, 2006)

"Simply Genius": My Life in Music, Science, and Global Renewal

(Hay House, 2011; McArthur, 2011)

ERVIN LASZLO

CHAOS POINT
2012 AND BEYOND

Foreword by Barbara Marx Hubbard

Our Choices Between

GLOBAL DISASTER
and a

SUSTAINABLE PLANET

APPOINTMENT WITH DESTINY

HR *for the evolving human spirit*

HAMPTON ROADS
PUBLISHING COMPANY, INC.

Originally published as *The Chaos Point* in 2006, ISBN: 1-57174-485-1.

Cover design: Laura Beers
Production Editor: Michele Kimble
Cover art © janrysavy/iStockphoto.com

Hampton Roads Publishing Company, Inc.
Charlottesville, VA 22906
www.hrpub.com

Library of Congress Cataloging-in-Publication Data available upon request.

ISBN: 978-1-57174-642-9
10 9 8 7 6 5 4 3 2 1

Printed on acid-free paper in the United States of America

CONTENTS

Chaos in modern systems theory defines the state of a system in which its stable cycles and processes give way to complex, seemingly unordered behavior, governed by so-called strange or chaotic attractors. In this state, the system is responsive even to tiny, sometimes immeasurably small fluctuations.

A *chaos-window*—in the human-context "decision-window"—is a transitory period in the evolution of a system during which any input or influence, however small, can "blow up" to change existing trends and bring new trends and processes into existence.

A *chaos point,* in turn, is the crucial tipping point in the evolution of a system in which trends that have brought the system to its present state break down and it can no longer return to its prior states and modes of behavior: It is launched irreversibly on a new trajectory that leads either to breakdown or to breakthrough to a new structure and a new mode of operation.

The Club of Budapest

The Club of Budapest, founded in 1993 by Ervin Laszlo, is an informal association of globally, as well as locally, active opinion leaders in various fields of art, science, religion, and culture, dedicated to the evolution of our values, ethics, and consciousness in the interest of averting a global crisis and creating a peaceful and sustainable civilization. It publishes books and reports, conducts surveys, awards prizes, and is creating a network of likeminded organizations, as well as a series of publications.

The Honorary Members of the Club of Budapest

Jose Arguelles, anthropologist

Oscar Arias, statesman/ Nobel Peace laureate

A. T. Ariyaratne, Buddhist spiritual leader

Deepak Chopra, physician, spiritual leader

The Fourteenth Dalai Lama, statesman/spiritual leader

Riane Eisler, feminist historian/activist

Vigdis Finnbogadottir, political leader

Milos Forman, film director

Peter Gabriel, musician

Rivka Golani, musician

Arpád Göncz, writer/statesman

Jane Goodall, scientist/activist

Mikhail Gorbachev, political leader

Václav Havel, writer/ statesman

Hazel Henderson, activist/economist

Jean Houston, spiritual leader

Barbara Marx Hubbard, futurist, activist

Bianca Jagger, human rights and environmental activist

Miklós Jancsó, film director

Ken-Ichiro Kobayashi, orchestra director

Gidon Kremer, musician

Prof. Shu-Hsien Liu, philosopher

Eva Marton, opera singer

Federico Mayor, scientist/activist

Zubin Mehta, orchestra director

Edgar Mitchell, scientist/astronaut

Edgar Morin, philosopher/sociologist

Robert Muller, educator/ activist

Gillo Pontecorvo, film director

Mary Robinson, political and human rights leader

Peter Russell, philosopher/ futurist

Karan Singh, statesman, Hindu spiritual leader

Sir Sigmund Sternberg, interfaith spiritual leader

Rita Süssmuth, political leader

Liv Ullmann, film actress/director

Richard von Weizsäcker, statesman

Elie Wiesel, writer/Nobel Peace laureate

Betty Williams, activist/ Nobel Peace laureate

Prof. Muhammad Yunus, economist/financial leader

FOREWORD

by Barbara Marx Hubbard

Ervin Laszlo is calling us to what may well be the greatest conscious moment in our collective experience as Homo sapiens sapiens. It is the first time that a species on this Earth has ever been aware that it could render itself extinct by its own actions. Or evolve itself toward an immeasurable future—also by its own actions.

This is the great wake-up call for human maturation. We have entered the first phase of conscious evolution, the evolution of evolution from unconscious to conscious choice, when our species becomes aware of the whole evolutionary journey and becomes co-responsible for guiding the process on a planetary scale.

Chaos Point 2012 and Beyond is of inestimable value because it situates us in this precise moment of evolutionary choice as a species and presents to us our options in the great drama of Conscious Evolution or Devolution and self-destruction.

As Laszlo writes, we live today in the very brief time of a "Chaos-window: a transitory period in the evolution of a system during which any input, however small, can 'blow up' to change existing trends and bring new trends and processes into existence." At a Chaos Point, "a system is launched irreversibly on a new trajectory that leads either to breakdown or to breakthrough to a new structure and new mode of operation."

Jonas Salk described this situation as a dangerous transition between Epoch A, our current precipitous set of crises leading to some form of collapse of human civilization; and Epoch B, a sustainable, regenerative, evolving future. We can envision such a positive future, we can yearn for it, work toward it. But how do we consciously "jump the gap" from Epoch A to Epoch B in time to avoid collapse, during the chaos-window, which we have never experienced before and have no experts on the process! No one has been educated in how to evolve a planet.

According to Laszlo,

> This Chaos Point will be reached when critical processes—conflicts and stresses in society, inequality in the distribution of resources in the economy, and the degeneration of vital balances in the ecology—reach a phase of irreversibility. Our systems will be launched on a trajectory either toward breakdown or toward breakthrough. Which trajectory will be selected is not determined in advance; the current decision-window has a high degree of indeterminacy, and hence of autonomy.

> This is due to the presence of consciousness. Conscious members of the social system can grasp the nature of the evolutionary processes that unfold around them and can purposefully intervene. At a decision-window, individuals can consciously create the small, but potentially powerful fluctuations that could "blow up" and decide the evolutionary path their society will adopt. They can tip the system toward the evolution that is in line with their hopes and expectations.

In brilliant descriptions of both the scenarios of breakdown and breakthrough, Laszlo gives us the guidelines we need to shift our consciousness and creativity toward the new civilization already emerging in our midst.

In this Foreword I would like to focus attention on the critical question which this book raises so dramatically: What can we do to actually get through this very short time frame of the chaos-window?

In a birth analogy, it is as if the new humanity is on the delivery table. We see the dangers of a failed birth, and the opportunities for our growth once we get through the birth canal. But as planetary midwives, what can we do to make sure we get through these next few years without massive further destruction of Earth Life?

Given the evolutionary reality of this very short time frame for transformation, let's imagine and enact a scenario that could actually get us through the chaos-window in time. Of course no one knows for sure how this happens, yet here is an educated assumption of what we can do together that is already almost happening.

I believe there are two vital factors to focus on:

One: Enhancing Social Synergy to connect and communicate what is breaking through out of what is breaking down.

Two: Fostering the Great Convergence of what is Emergent in the December 2010 to 2012 time frame and beyond.

This time frame, as Lazlo describes, has both a multi-faceted prophetic and scientific basis. Even more important, this window in time is already attracting large-scale public interest and events. It can be built upon to jump us through the chaos-window through massive coherence and connectivity of the positive.

The combination of enhanced Social Synergy/communication and the Convergence of the Emergent by 2012 may be natural elements of the evolutionary formula required to foster *non-linear exponential interaction of what is already working* toward the new civilization.

First of all, how can we speed up social synergy in time? There are already many groups working toward social synergy, social innovations, and various forms of collaboration and positive media. They can make the effort to synergize among themselves until we have a synthesis of that which is synergizing.

We also need a meta-innovation on the Internet that connects and communicates innovations already arising in every field and function. A name for this meta-innovation to support all innovations is the Synergy Engine. The evolutionary function of the Synergy Engine on the Internet (a next step after the search engines) is to scan for, map, connect, and communicate what is working, to mobilize for effective action, based on our growing capacities in every field.*

Ervin Laszlo tells us, "The formation of higher-level 'suprasystems' through the interlinking of previously relatively autonomous systems . . . Physicist Manfred Eigen has shown that suprasystem-formation through auto- and cross-catalytic cycles is the basis of evolution of all life on the planet."

The Synergy Engine is being conceived as such a suprasystem, capable of scaling up to facilitate millions of people to connect, to cocreate, to seek common

*The Synergy Engine is now in development through the Foundation for Conscious Evolution and its partners, with the intention of being ready on or before December 2012.

goals and match needs with resources within fields of endeavor, across fields, and within the system as a whole.

It becomes an associative memory system for our planet, replete with information and knowledge of our successes, breakthroughs and potentials. An emergent property itself, it springs from the genius of the information and communication advances of the last decades. Eventually, it is hoped, it will become a "Global Peace Room" as sophisticated as our war rooms, to track innovation and success against our common enemies of hunger, environmental destruction, poverty, and war, while fostering global coherence and connection through the heart.

As the astronauts gave us the first pictures of Earth from space and changed our view of the world, so the Synergy Engine will be designed to reflect the whole system shift already underway. It would help make the invisible visible, giving us continuing "alive" pictures of our emerging creativity and goodness, in all its beauty and magnificence, and thereby attract us forward together.

A second factor in which we can all assist, and which could lead to a quantum jump, is a Great Convergence of Celebrations—planned already leading up to and for 2012—that is growing every day. Teilhard de Chardin pointed out that "Everything that rises converges." What if we hold the intention and develop the process to connect and synergize all the efforts being made to celebrate 2012, aiming together at a quantum shift in consciousness on a global scale?

As Laszlo notes,

> The famous—or infamous—date, "21 December 2012"—is on the horizon, and there are many indications that this date—or at least the period around it—will indeed be decisive. It will mark the "tipping point" beyond which the current world, with its institutions, lifestyles, values, and behaviors will no longer be viable: civilization as we know it will not be further sustainable.

Many such celebrations are already being planned. Ervin Laszlo's Club of Budapest, through its newly forming international branch, the Club of Budapest International (COBI), and the affiliated WorldShift 2012 organizations, are among the leading advocates of such celebrations. Their activities include a new WorldShift Alliance of enlightened organizations and committed individuals and WorldShift Media & Events, a new social enterprise providing a global and fully integrated multi-media communications platform promoting the goals of member organizations of the WorldShift Alliance, including peace, justice, sustainability, social innovation, and conscious evolution. A series of global macro-micro events will focus world attention on WorldShift Days. These will be 10/10/10; 11/11/11; and 12/21/12. The affiliated projects include the ambitious and exciting Temple of Light/Story of Humanity event in Jerusalem on 12/21/12.

Jose Argüelles, whose work is described in this book, writes,

> We are promoting and planning a rolling harmonic convergence throughout the 2012 year until we get to the peak experience point 12/21/2012. There will be many events and we want to see that they all get hooked up so they present a conscious moving matrix in time, connecting all the light points of the terrestrial grid. Among other things we are calling for galactic synchronization ground crews of no less than three members to establish themselves at select sacred sites in reparation for telepathic intervention.

Another world-shifting event is initiated by Michael Tanner, "Day One 2012":

> From the Phoenix base site, we wish to network and interact with events around the globe, weaving our own enabling, advanced technology showcase (featuring demonstration and simulation of zero point and fusion energy systems), conferences, exhibits, and multimedia presentations to empower change for the planet. The centerpiece of all of this will be the Theater for the Future journey with the presentation of "Day One" multi-segment experience and its culminating planetary birthing moment for all to share in and participate, all signaling the advent of a New Calendar with infinite possibilities for the future. This is intended to call forth a massive synchronicity and focus our collective consciousness to contribute to an actual shift in the field of Earth, raising our own consciousness to meet whatever is higher within us and beyond us.

Another vital initiative is called FourYears.Go. Springing out of the Pachemama Alliance and supported by a major New York advertising firm, it is drawing together thousands of people and organizations to aim within the next four years for an actual shift of consciousness and behavior on a planetary scale.

Many other important events, books, and videos are coming forward, calling us to the 2012 time frame of possibilities and opportunities.

When we add to all of this the vital activities of GATE: Global Alliance for Transformational Entertainment, drawn together by John Raatz and other media innovators, inviting media professionals to join together with visionaries to support each other in creating powerful new media for our conscious evolution, we may have the evolutionary mix that shifts our world in time . . . and what else, if not this, is worth trying, anyway!

We need now a Planetary Call—calling everyone—to participate in what can be the greatest set of events in the history of the world, a planetary evolution that is consciously co-created by and for humanity. Such a Call is now arising as global voices for our conscious evolution are being heard throughout the world.

How this will unfold we do not know exactly. Herein lies the drama. I come back to the metaphor of birth. It is as if an infant were having trouble getting though the birth canal. If it and its mother did not know about birth, they would think that it is dying. It is in fact dying to the old womb-phase of growth and consciousness. The Call lets us know that Our Crisis is a Birth. It is the Birth of what is emerging for humanity. The strange truth is that we must become midwives to ourselves!

It is during this chaos-window that the promise of Ervin Laszlo's great life work may be fulfilled. His intention for WorldShift2012 is not only brilliant, it is causal. This book, as well as his other recent books including *WorldShift 2012,* and *Quantum Shift in the Global Brain* are helping us to make it through together. The vital councils and organizations he has helped to form, such as the original Club of Budapest, and most recently the Club of Budapest International, serve as fundamental evolutionary awakeners in the present chaos-window.*

We are the generation privileged to become conscious of evolutionary transformation and aware of our vital role within it. This is comparable to humanity's coming of age at the dawn of self-reflective consciousness 30,000 years ago. We are gaining evolutionary consciousness and are jointly creating the Evolutionary Potential Movement with the promise of nurturing a co-evolving, co-creative universal humanity. Holding before us the vision of the "strange attractor" of ourselves as a spiritually, socially and scientifically evolving species, may indeed be the vital magnet we need to pull us through the birthing process that Ervin Laszlo names the chaos-window.

---

*www.clubofbudapest.org

PREFACE

This book was not created intentionally; certainly, I never intended to write it. As Topsy, it was not born, it just grew. *That* it did is worth noting, because it could throw light on *why* it did—and that in turn could tell us something about the world we live in today.

During most of the year 2000 and for the first months of 2001, I was working on a book titled *Macroshift: Navigating the Transformation to a Sustainable World*. It was published by a reputable San Francisco-based publisher in the first week of September 2001. Like the present book, it attempted to grasp the nature of the transformation we are living through and offer thoughts on how to orient it into a humanly desirable direction. It contained strongly worded statements regarding the futility of war and the use of national armies, even for defense, not to mention for the kind of aggression that subsequently became known as "preventive warfare." A few days later, 9/11 happened. The book was received with massive silence: as far as I know, not a single discussion or review appeared of it in the United States. But it was translated into various foreign languages (Dutch, French, German, Portuguese-Brazilian, Russian, Turkish, as well as Chinese and Japanese), and it did well elsewhere: in Germany it was named best futures book of the year 2003.

In the fall of 2004, friends and associates who read the original edition suggested that it should appear in a new edition since the ideas it offered could now be discussed. Their relevance, rather than having diminished with the passage of time, had actually heightened. At the end of January 2005 I sat down to review the text and see where it needed updating. I reviewed the statistical data and inserted the latest available figures—this was easy, since I had the text on my computer—and sent the revised version to my good friend and literary agent Bill Gladstone of Waterside Productions. He was to contact the San Francisco publisher as well as other houses and see who was interested in bringing it out. Thinking that, as far as I was concerned, this took care of the matter, I turned to my other commitments.

But this was not the end of it. A few days later a research report someone sent me by e-mail gave information that I felt would be well to insert, so I went back to the text and inserted it. In the weeks and months that followed this happened not once, but more and more frequently. Somehow, the data and reports I needed appeared with amazing regularity on my computer. Further materials came to hand during meetings and discussions, and inserting them became almost a full-time job. People who had no knowledge of what I was about, talked to me about the problems I was dealing with and came up with relevant ideas and source materials. In consequence, what started out as a revised and updated edition of *Macroshift* turned into *The Chaos Point*, a substantially new book.

Now at the dawn of the second decade of the twenty-first century, both the time and the opportunity had come to update what I had written earlier. The main body of the text does not require changing; it is as valid and timely today as it was the day it was committed to paper. But the coming of the chaos point has become more visible, and also closer. The famous—or infamous—date, "21 December 2012," is on the horizon, and there are many indications that this date—or at least the period around it—will indeed be decisive. It will mark the "tipping point" beyond which the current world, with its institutions, lifestyles, values, and behaviors, will no longer be viable: civilization as we know it will not be further sustainable. I have added a chapter to outline why the chaos point is now so close and what it means for people in every part of the world—ourselves and our seemingly privileged parts included. It is essential to overcome the remaining pockets of skepticism that wish (understandably) to dismiss the entire concept of a chaos or tipping point by reason of fear, or simply due to complacency. The facts speak clearly, and should be allowed to speak. It's time to wake up: the time for effective action is running out.

I hope that this new edition of *Chaos Point* will serve as a clarion call to wake up, to pay attention, and to start to act. Our future, and that of our children, hangs in the balance.

Spring 2010

PROLOGUE

Two Paths to the Future

A Chinese proverb warns, "If we do not change direction, we are likely to end up exactly where we are headed." Applied to contemporary humanity, this would be disastrous. Without a change in direction, we are on the way to a world of increasing population pressure and poverty; growing potential for social and political conflict; escalating maverick and organized warfare; accelerating climate change; food, water, and energy shortages; worsening industrial, urban, and agricultural pollution; further destruction of the ozone layer; accelerating reduction of biodiversity; and continued loss of atmospheric oxygen. We also run the risk of mega-disasters caused by nuclear accidents and leaking nuclear waste, devastating floods and tornadoes due to climate change, and widespread health problems owing to natural catastrophes as well as to such human factors as the accumulation of toxins in soil, air, and water.

Where we are now headed is not where we want to go.

- Current world population is about 6.6 billion people and is increasing at the rate of 90 million a year. The U.N. forecast calls for 7.85 billion by 2025 and 8.92 billion by 2050. The world population quadrupled in the course of the twentieth century, and doubled between 1960 and 2000 alone.
- Wealth and wellbeing are increasingly unequally distributed in the population. Eighty percent of the world's domestic product belongs to one billion people, and the remaining 20 percent is shared by five-and-a-half billion people. Twenty percent of the global population (about 1.3 billion people) consumes

86 percent of the world's resources; nearly half of the world's population (three billion people) subsist on less than $2 a day, while the richest 10 percent (650 million people) has 54 percent of the global income. These imbalances will only worsen, since the poor countries are paying $38 billion more each year in interest than they are receiving in development aid.

- In developing countries, one out of every three children is undernourished, and over 11 million children under five die annually of preventable diseases and inadequate nutrition.
- One in three urban dwellers in the world live in slums, shantytowns, favelas, and urban ghettoes—more than 900 million people are classified as slum-dwellers. In the poorest countries 78% of the urban population subsists under life-threatening circumstances.
- Although more women and girls are being educated than in previous years, in many parts of the world fewer women have jobs and more are forced to make ends meet in the "informal sector."
- There is a greater propensity in many parts of the world for resorting to terrorism and other forms of violence to right wrongs, or at least to call attention to the perceived wrongs. There is deepening insecurity in countries both rich and poor.
- Islamic fundamentalism is spreading throughout the Muslim world, neo-Nazi and other extremist movements are surfacing in Europe, and religious fanaticism is appearing the world over.
- As some governments seek to contain maverick violence through organized warfare, conflicts heat up in the Middle East, Asia, Central America, and other hot spots.
- In 2005, world military spending rose for a sixth year running, growing by 5 percent to $1.04 trillion. High-income countries account for three-fourths of world military spending while they have less than 16 percent of the world's population. The United States spends $455 billion a year on military and defense applications, almost half the world figure. The G8 countries together sell over $12 billion in arms to the poorest countries.
- There is a drop in food self-sufficiency in the majority of the world's economies, ominously coupled with the diminution of the internationally available food reserves.
- There is also a diminution of available freshwater for well over half of the world's population; 1.1 billion people lack safe drinking water.

- Vital balances are continually degrading in the world's atmosphere, in the oceans and freshwater systems, and in productive soils. Half of the world's forests have already disappeared, and the loss continues at the rate of 9.4 million hectares a year. Species extinction increases at a staggering rate, accelerated by habitat-destruction and climate change. Up to one-third of all the species alive today may become extinct by 2100. The consequences include the greenhouse effect with attendant climate change, and a reduction of the productivity of seas, lakes, rivers, and agricultural lands. Some processes feed on themselves and are already out of control: As the Arctic ice melts, the sea absorbs more warmth which makes for more melting; as Siberian permafrost disappears the methane released from the peat-bog below exacerbates the greenhouse effect and makes for more melting and thus for more methane.

There are persistently worrisome trends in the world's richest country and sole remaining superpower.

- Poverty and hunger have been on the rise. According to official measures of poverty, in the year 2003, 12.5 percent of the total U.S. population lived in poverty; 10 million households—31 million individuals, of whom 12 million were children—risked hunger or faced food insecurity; and 3.1 million households—including 2 million children—suffered from actual hunger.
- As the aftermath of hurricane Katrina has shown, the poorest segment of the U.S. population is continually neglected as the Administration assigns funds and gives priority to fighting for economic interests abroad rather than securing decent living conditions for the poor at home. Environmental objectives that could interfere with economic growth are persistently sidestepped.
- The richest segment of the population has been becoming still richer, but wealth has failed to ensure financial security: a poll of the U.S. Private Bank showed that 64 percent of rich Americans with an average wealth of $38 million feel financially insecure.
- In the name of safeguarding national security, increasing restrictions have been placed on civil liberties, including free speech and freedom of expression in the press and on the Internet, and individuals suspected of being a security threat were detained without trial and at times subjected to torture.

If such trends continue, we shall be launched on a path not just to national, but to global breakdown.

A Scenario of Breakdown

Global breakdown begins in the poorest regions, most directly exposed to the negative effects of climate change:

Changing weather patterns create drought, flooding, devastating storms and widespread harvest failures;

Coastal areas are flooded by rising sea levels;

Health conditions in mega-city environments as well as in rural backwaters are critically deteriorated because of the accumulation of toxins in soil, air, and water;

Harvests are cut back due to the exhaustion of nutrients in artifically overexploited soils;

Areas dependent on adequate rainfall for food production and exposed to tornados, hurricanes and violent storms experience growing famine.

Massive waves of migration get under way from the threatened regions to areas where resources seem more assured.

The breakdown of the poorest and most directly exposed regions spreads over the continents and creates a global security threat.

Rural residents dependent on local natural resources become poorer while powerful elites control, and are likely to extract exorbitant profits from, increasingly valuable forests, land, and water.

People pressed into poverty and left without adequate means of survival join rebellions against local landowners and government officials;

Epidemics of infectious diseases spread over Africa, Asia, and the Americas owing to heat waves, outbreaks of agricultural pests, and contaminated drinking water;

Massive waves of migration to the relatively well-off regions overload the local resource base and create conflict with the established populations;

Terrorist groups, nuclear proliferators, narco-traffickers, and organized crime form alliances with unscrupulous entrepreneurs and expand the scale and scope of their activities, carrying out suicide bombings, corrupting leaders, infiltrating troubled banks and businesses, and cooperating with insurgents to control more and more territory. Traffic in narcotics, hazardous wastes, and toxic materials joins traffic in illicit biological, chemical, and nuclear weapons;

Global security reaches a critical low-point.

In country after country strong military and police measures create a high level of perceived as well as real repression, and contribute to the increase of frustration and resentment. A vicious cycle is created that feeds on itself.

In the relatively affluent parts of the world the rapid rise in military expenditures diverts money from health and environmental care, aggravates the plight of poor populations and worsens the condition of the environment. There is deepening conflict between the remaining groups of haves and the growing segments of have-nots.

Governments are under mounting pressure; one after the other resorts to military measures to shore up crumbling borders, ensure access to basic resources for their people, and "cleanse" territories of unwanted populations. In the most heavily hit countries military might is concentrated in the hands of power brokers, dictators, and juntas.

The "war on terror" engulfs entire populations, ignites civil wars, and catalyzes further acts of terrorism. Before long, power-hungry, fearful, or simply unscrupulous leaders resort to the use of weapons of mass destruction, including nuclear arms. As in country after country social, economic, and environmental crisis is met with military countermeasures, war and violence escalate, and the global system breaks down.

Trends are not destiny: They can be changed. Breakdown is just one of the possible futures before us. We are not yet definitively launched on its path. If we wake up to the need to cope with the dangers we face and join a sense of urgency to live and act responsibly with a sense of commitment to each other and to our shared future we can still shift to a path of breakthrough.

The Scenario of Breakthrough

Faced with growing problems and shared threats, concerned groups of citizens pull together, form associations and networks, and pursue shared objectives of peace and sustainability.

Business leaders recognize the groundswell of change in the thinking and expectations of their clients and customers and respond with goods and services that meet the shift in demand.

Global news and entertainment media explore fresh perspectives and emerging social and cultural innovations. A new vision of self, others, and nature surfaces on the Internet, on television, and in the communication networks of enterprises, communities, and ethnic groups.

In consequence, a new culture of responsibility and solidarity emerges in society. There is growing support for public policies that manifest social and ecological concern. Funds and capital are channeled from military and defense applications to the needs of the people who make up the bulk of society. Measures are implemented to safeguard the environment, create an effective system of food and resource distribution, and develop and put to work sustainable energy, transport, and agricultural technologies.

More and more people gain access to food, jobs, and education. More and more enter on the Internet as active dialogue partners. Their communication reinforces solidarity and uncovers win-win areas where mutual interests can be jointly promoted.

Decision-makers in the sphere of national and international economics shift their operating principles from living on "natural capital" to living on "natural income." (Natural capital consists of the accumulated riches of the earth, used and discarded, as in the burning of fossil fuels. When such capital is depleted, the economic systems based on it go bankrupt—they are unsustainable. Natural income, on the other hand, consists of the almost infinitely available resources of nature—above all, solar radiation—and of efficiently and effectively replenishable and recyclable resources. Economic systems living off natural income are intrinsically sustainable.)

In the business world a corresponding shift obtains in regard to the way natural resources are employed. The emerging objective is not to optimize labor-productivity (which has been the principal goal and preoccupation of business for most of the twentieth century), but to increase the level of resource-productivity. This means designing production processes and creating consumer goods so as to use the least amount of nonrenewable resources and maximize the share of indefinitely available or recyclable resources.

Supported by these developments, national, international and intercultural mistrust, ethnic conflict, racial oppression, economic inequity, and gender inequality gives way to mutual trust and respect, and a readiness to form partnerships and cooperate. Rather than breaking down in conflict and war, humanity breaks through to a sustainable world of self-reliant but cooperating communities, enterprises, states, and regions.

Which path will we take in the coming years? The answer is not in yet; we still have a window of time. But the window is closing; the chaos point is approaching. It may come as soon as the end of 2012.

Chaos Point 2012

There is a growing wave of thinking that associates the coming of a chaos point with the famous end of 2012 date. Some people contest this assumption and go as far as to claim that all talk of a chaos point is mistaken; the world as it is today will not change, at least not in our lifetime. Others take the contrary view, claiming that it's already too late: the chaos point has already been passed. This is the view expressed by James Lovelock, the British scientist who, thirty years ago, worked out how the Earth possesses a planetary-scale control system that keeps it fit for life (the "Gaia hypothesis"). Lovelock maintains that the "Gaia system" is out of control. "I think we have little option," he wrote in *The Revenge of Gaia,* "but to prepare for the worst, and assume that we have passed the threshold. The Earth's physical condition must be seen as seriously ill and soon to pass into a morbid fever that may last as long as 100,000 years." The principal reason for this pessimistic assessment is global warming. The heating up of the atmosphere will create "a hell of a climate." The average temperature will rise 8 degrees centigrade in temperate regions and 5 degrees in the tropics.

Is Lovelock right—have we reached a catastrophic chaos point already? When we take a closer look at his argument, we find room for a more positive assessment. Lovelock's reasoning about the dynamics of the Earth's physical-biological systems is sound, but he doesn't recognize that not only nature, but also humanity is a dynamic system on the threshold of a chaos point. Human societies, much like planetary ecologies, are not infinitely stressable. Sooner or later they reach a point at which they tip one way or another. When that chaos point is reached, they become ultra-sensitive and capable of rapid transformation. The dangers as well as the opportunities conveyed by chaos points apply to natural as well as to human systems.

Will the coming of a chaos point in human societies coincide with the famous 2012 prophecies? Many people say so, but such claims need to be substantiated. For the most part, they refer to traditional and highly esoteric prophecies. Is there also scientific evidence to back them up?

The Prophecies

The most famous of the prophecies that speak of the end of 2012 as a critical point in human life and civilization is undoubtedly that of the Mayans. The Mayans viewed civilization as a cyclic process, where shifts from one phase of the cycle to the next occur at specific intervals.

This cyclic concept of the world was not unique to the Mayans. Cycles exist everywhere in nature and have been recognized in almost all cultures. In the biosphere some cycles are daily, others seasonal or annual. Roughly 24-hour circadian cycles govern many of our bodily functions in accordance with the alternation of day and night. Menstrual cycles average 28 days, and the ebb and flow of tidal waters reflect the changing positions of the Moon and Sun relative to the Earth. Solar cycles displayed by the frequency of sunspots last about 11 years, with the solar maximum and solar minimum recurring in each cycle.

Cycles have been perceived in history as well. They were seen as the advent and passing of "Great Ages." These include the astrological Great Year, which lasts just under 26 thousand years (based on the precession of the equinoxes), and the Yuga of Hindu philosophy, a specific epoch within the cycle of four ages: Satya, Treta, Dvapara, and Kali. Numerous myths speak of celestial cycles, and many civilizations have attempted to map their principal transitions. Celestial calendars have been a major reference for life in traditional civilizations. One of the most famous of these calendars is the Tzolk'in calendar, a 260-day Mesoamerican system that was known to the Mayans.

Some modern historians, among them Arnold Toynbee and Pitirim Sorokin, advanced a cyclic interpretation of history. Toynbee viewed civilization as a movement rather than a condition, exhibiting a "life cycle" in which eight years is the period of gestation, eighty the period of physical self-expression, and 800 the total life-span.

The Mayan's interpretation of history is embedded in their calendar, completed by priest-astronomers in the year 1479 and carved into the Aztec-Mayan sun stone. The Mayan calendar details long passages of time, and includes mathematical calculations so accurate that modern astronomers are at a loss to understand how a traditional people could arrive at them.

The relevant calculation is the so-called long count. The "Age of Jaguar," the thirteenth *baktun* of 144,000 days, will come to an end on the 21st of December, 2012. That will mark the end of the Fourth Sun—also known as the Fourth World—and the shift to a new era. The Mayan calendar doesn't predict that with the end of the Fourth World the world itself will come to an end. Rather, December 21, 2012 will be a date of rebirth, the beginning of the World of the Fifth Sun.

The Mayan's prediction of world transformation at the end of 2012 is not unique: astrologers have arrived at the same conclusion on the basis of their own system. They have noted that at sunrise on December 21, 2012, the Sun will conjunct the intersection of the Milky Way and the plane of the ecliptic, creating a cosmic cross. The center of our galaxy will complete a "cosmic year": a 25,920-year journey around the wheel of the zodiac. According to most systems of astrology, a new cosmic year will then begin, lasting for another 25,920 years. (An astronomical, rather than astrological, account of this cycle concerns the rotation of the Earth on its axis. It's about 23 degrees off vertical: our planet is like a spinning top that is slightly out of balance. Given this condition, it takes 25,800 years for the celestial pole to describe a full circle.)

The cosmic conjunction occurs in a thirty-six-year window in time between 1980 and 2016. This was known to the Mayans, but they appear to have deliberately chosen 2012 as the significant point, even though it's not in the middle of this window. At the 2012 winter solstice, the Earth's axis will be pointing exactly toward the "galactic bulge"—the thick central part of our galaxy. This was seen as the time of a fundamental re-alignment by other spiritual traditions as well, including the Hopi time-keeping system, Vedic and Islamic astrology, Mithraism, the Jewish kabala, European sacred geography, medieval Christian architecture, and a variety of hermetic metaphysics.

Mystical philosopher Terence McKenna arrived at the 2012 date on the basis of mathematical calculations based on the *I Ching*. McKenna's "timewave" takes account of the ebb and flow of novelty in the universe. The great periods of novelty began about four billion years ago when the planet was formed, and continued sixty-five million years before our time, when the dinosaurs became extinct and mammals diffused over the continents. There was a surge of novelty between 15,000 and 8,000 B.C.E., the approximate period of the Neolithic Revolution and the birth of agriculture with settled communities. Another surge occurred around 500 B.C.E. when Lao-Tzu, Plato, Zoroaster, Buddha, and other seminal figures appeared on the stage of history. The calculation yields further novelty waves in the late eighteenth century, at the epoch of social and scientific revolutions, in the turbulent 1960s, and in the early twenty-first century, coinciding with the time of the 9/11 terrorist attack. The next peak of novelty fell in November of 2008, which was the date of the transformative U.S. elections, and another wave is to occur in October of 2010. The waves are to culminate on the twenty-first of December, 2012. At that point novelty is to reach infinity—anything and everything conceivable to the mind could then occur at the same time.

The Evidence

What independent evidence do we have that the 2012 prophecies harbor an element of truth? Are there scientifically established grounds to believe that the end of 2012 will mark a global tipping point for humanity?

First of all, we should know what a chaos or tipping point means in the context of science. We review this question in the Postscript, and merely highlight the principal points here.

The disciplines known collectively as the systems sciences (general systems and general evolution theory, chaos theory, cybernetics, information and complexity theory, and nonequilibrium thermodynamics, among others) describe a tipping point as a state of chaos in a system. At that point, so-called "chaotic" or "strange" attractors replace more stable point or periodic attractors in the system's "phase portrait," and the new attractors induce chaotic behavior in the system. This is not behavior that lacks order and is merely random; it is finely ordered behavior governed by mathematically described attractors. This makes the system's functioning complex as well as sensitive. In such conditions even small changes—whether they occur in the system's environment, or within the system—produce major effects: the so-called "butterfly" effects. In a condition of chaos, the system is ultrasensitive, and prone to sudden change and transformation.

There is evidence that the systems of life on this planet approach a chaos point. Weather patterns turn extreme over the whole world. The changes range from droughts in China and Australia, floods in North America, increased cyclone activity, to devastating hurricanes that impact tropical coastlines and move inland. Threats to health surface on a scale never before experienced: avian flu and "novel swine flu," malaria, and other tropical diseases believed to have been vanquished. Global warming creates a widespread and frequent incidence of vector-borne diseases such as malaria and dengue fever, as well as of water-borne diseases such as cholera.

Climate change is a major factor of stress in the contemporary world, but not the only factor. The record shows global and local temperatures strongly fluctuating. The average is rising: in the summer of 2003 temperature fluctuations averaged 2.3 degrees higher than in previous years. Globally, temperatures have risen over the past century by at least $0.74°C$, and the principal causes are still debated. More than likely, both human and natural processes conspire to produce the warming. It is known that greenhouse gases in the Earth's atmosphere trap the sun's rays and heat up the atmosphere. This is bound to be a factor in global warming, whether or not changes in the physical processes of the Sun contribute to the warming.

Global warming is also produced by natural causes. As well as the emission of CO_2 and other greenhouses gases, variations in the sun's radiation and in sunspot activity, variations in the Earth's orbit and spin, and volcanic geo-thermal activity affect and warm the planet's troposphere and stratosphere.

In its 2007 report, the Intergovernmental Panel on Climate Change (IPCC) declared that the warming of the world's climate is now "unequivocal." This is a matter of observed fact. It comes to the fore in the increase of temperatures in the arctic, in the reduced size of icebergs and the melting of icecaps and glaciers, in the reduction of areas under permafrost, in changes in rainfall patterns, and in new wind formations, droughts, heat waves, tropical cyclones and other extreme weather patterns.

The consequences of global warming include widespread flooding due to tropical storms and the rise of sea levels. The melting of the Greenland icecap could alter the flow of the Gulf Stream and may deflect it before it reaches the European continent, dropping temperatures in England and the Nordic countries to levels typical of Labrador. If the West Antarctic ice sheet disintegrated, during this century the level of the sea would rise by meters and not centimeters, and human settlements close to sea level would be inundated.

According to the Stern Review, commissioned by the British government in 2007, there is a 50 percent risk of global temperatures rising by more than 5°C by the year 2100. In a conservative formulation, this would create a "5 to 20 percent reduction in consumption levels" worldwide. But even a global temperature increase of 3°C would radically transform the flows and balances of the ecology on which animal, plant, and human life is now vitally dependent.

Global stress is further induced by the growth of the world's population. At the end of the twentieth century population was growing by about 900 million per decade, equivalent to a new London every month. It passed 6 billion before the turn of the century, and demographic calculations indicate that it will reach 9.1 billion by the middle of the twenty-first century. Urban dwellers number more than half of the world's population, and U.N. forecasts speak of 60 percent of the global population living in cities by 2030.

Modern cities are the largest conglomerations of humans ever seen on this planet. There are mega-conglomerations such as the Greater Tokyo area, with 35 million inhabitants, and Sao Paolo, with 23 or 25 million. Other cities are rapidly catching up: Mumbai, Delhi, Mexico City, Dhaka, Jakarta, and Lagos, among others. By 2015 there may be 23 mega-cities in the world, 19 of them in the developing world, and 37 cities with populations between 5 and 10 million.

Rapid urbanization in developing countries exposes vast numbers of poor people to shortages of drinking water and sanitation, as well as to rising air pollution and air-borne toxins. Large cities produce enormous social inequalities; over one billion people now squat in squalor in slums, favelas and bidonvilles.

Urban overcrowding and sub-minimal conditions of life in urban conglomerations are major factors that stress people in many parts of the world. They produce frustration and conflict, resulting in higher levels of violence and unusual forms of crime: mass murders when seemingly ordinary people run amok, renewed suicide bombing in populated city centers, and suicidal terrorism on land and in the air.

The rapid growth of the world's population, especially the growth of cities, creates growing problems of energy. Urban centers consume three-quarters of the world's energy and are responsible for at least three-quarters of its pollution. The supply of abundant cheap energy has entered a critical end-phase. As the world continues to run on fossil fuels, demand for oil rises and supply diminishes. At the beginning of the second decade of the twenty-first century, most of the world's oil-producers had passed their peak. The largest oilfields were discovered over half a century ago: the peak of discovery was in 1965. New fields have not been found at the same rate, and as a result global oil production will peak, or has already peaked. As the peak is passed, oil becomes more difficult and expensive to extract. The supply of cheap oil drops, and extraction becomes less profitable. Yet demand for oil is still rising: the International Energy Agency found that in the last few years, global demand has been increasing by 2 million barrels a day. If no significant changes in the patterns of energy production and consumption come about, global demand for oil will rise in the next two decades, from the present 80 million barrels a day to 125 million barrels.

Growing demand and decreasing supply drives prices up. Surges in oil prices instantly impact people, enterprises, and economies in every part of the world. Higher prices also trigger conflict related to discovery and extraction. The Arctic Ocean seabed, which may hold billions of gallons of both oil and natural gas, is becoming a globally contested region. In March 2007, Russia made public that it plans to set up a military force to protect its interests in the Arctic, and in August of that year the Russian flag had been planted on the ocean bed 4 km beneath the North Pole to indicate Russia's claim to the undersea oil-formation known as the Lomonosov Ridge. The United Kingdom in turn is claiming sovereign rights over more than 1 million square kilometers (386,000 square miles) of the seabed off Antarctica. The opening up of the Northwest passage due to the melting of Arctic ice is already provoking international contestation and conflict.

Physical changes in the intensity of solar radiation conspire with anthropic impacts to create stress in the system. Astronomers have noted that since the 1940s, and particularly since 2003, the Sun has become remarkably turbulent. Solar activity is predicted to peak around 2012, creating storms of intensity unprecedented since the 1859 "Carrington event," when a large solar flare accompanied by a coronal mass ejection flung billions of tons of solar plasma into the Earth's magnetosphere.

Solar storms, capable of traveling at speeds of up to 5 million miles per hour, could knock out virtually every major technological infrastructure on the planet: transportation, security and emergency response systems, electricity grids, finance, telecommunications, including satellite and other wireless networks, and even household electronic equipment.

The solar storm of 1859 was the most powerful event of its kind in recorded history. On the 1st of September of that year, the Sun expelled huge quantities of high-energy protons in a large flare that traveled directly toward the Earth, taking eighteen hours instead of the usual three or four days to reach our planet. It disrupted telegraph systems all over Europe and North America. Fires erupted in telegraph stations due to power surges in the wires; and the northern lights (aurora borealis) were seen as far south as Florida.

The next solar storm on record, in March of 1989, melted the transformers of the HydroQuebec Power Grid, causing a nine-hour blackout that affected six million people in Canada. And the solar storms that reached the Earth between October 19th and November 7th, 2003, disrupted satellites and global communications, air travel, navigation systems, and power grids all over the world. It also affected systems on the International Space Station.

The solar maximum forecast for 2012 would do greater harm than any before, since human life has become more dependent on the global energy grid. According to "Severe Space Weather Events: Understanding Economic and Societal Impacts," a National Research Council report issued in the spring of 2009 by the U.S. National Academy of Sciences, another Carrington event would induce ground currents that knock out 300 key transformers within 90 seconds and cut off power for more than 130 million people in the U.S. alone. Its cost could be as high as 2 trillion dollars, and recovery time would be four to ten years. An even worse impact would be felt in China, where the electrical grid is more vulnerable than in the West.

A major solar storm would cause the failure of electric power in most parts of the world. The above cited report of the National Academy of Science claims that this would have catastrophic consequences. People in high-rise apartments, where water has to be pumped up, would be cut off immediately. For most others, drinking water would come through the taps for about half a day, but the flow would then cease without electricity to pump it from reservoirs. Transportation systems directly or indirectly dependent on electric power (which means practically all systems) would come to a standstill. Back-up generators would operate at some sites until their fuel ran out. For hospitals, that would mean about 72 hours of essential care only services. Without power for heating, cooling, and refrigeration, and with a breakdown in the distribution of medicines and pharmaceuticals, urban populations would begin to die within days.

Scientists forecast yet another disruptive event for the end of 2012: breaches in the Earth's magnetic field. In the past, this field protected living systems from the effects of solar storms and coronal mass ejections. Lately the magnetic field has diminished in intensity and holes and gaps have appeared. Scientists in South Africa measured cracks in the magnetic field the size of California, and in December of 2008 NASA announced that its Themis Project had found a massive breach that would allow devastating amounts of solar plasma to enter the Earth's magnetosphere.

The fluctuation of the magnetic field could also lead to the reversal of the planet's magnetic poles. During the course of reversal the magnetic field would become still weaker, and the danger to life from solar and stellar radiation would greatly increase.

Another scientific report of relevance concerns the entry of our solar system into a highly energized region of space. This turbulent region is making the Sun hotter and stormier, and has already caused climate change on other planets. According to Russian scientists, the effects on Earth will include an acceleration of the magnetic pole shift, the vertical and horizontal distribution of ozone, and an increase in the frequency and magnitude of extreme climate events.

Quite apart from mystical and esoteric prophecies, there is solid evidence that 2012 will be a turbulent period. Will we be ready for it—ready to cope with the disruptions, and to seize the opportunities that come in their wake?

PART ONE

THE TIDES OF TRANSFORMATION

I

New Thinking for a New World

Einstein told us that we cannot solve the significant problems we face at the same level of thinking at which we were when we created the problems. He was right: The problems we face today cannot be solved at the level of thinking that gave rise to them. Yet we are trying to do just that. We are fighting terrorism, poverty, criminality, cultural conflict, environmental degradation, ill health, even obesity and other "sicknesses of civilization" with the same kind of thinking—the same means and methods—that produced the problems in the first place. Two examples will make this clear.

Contemporary nation-states fight terrorism by tightening security. They fight not so much *terrorism* as *terrorists*. Terrorism, they say, is to be eliminated by preventing terrorists from carrying out their base projects, and the best way to do that is to hunt them down, put them in jail, or kill them—before they kill us. This strategy is analogous to attempting to cure an organism of cancer by cutting out the cancerous cells. The cure works if the organism is not affected beyond the group of cancerous cells, which is a fortunate case but not a common one. If the organism is affected, other cells turn cancerous and not only replace the ones that are surgically cut out but also spread. Ultimately, of course, they will kill the organism and thus also themselves. If we are to cure a body that produces cancer cells, we would do better to cure the body itself, rather than just cut out the malfunctioning cells. A proper cure means going beyond the logic of the cells that reproduce without constraint; it extends to the process that makes the cells reproduce this way in the first place.

Why do cells turn cancerous? The question is precisely analogous to: Why do people become terrorists? Heads of national security dismiss the question; they say that terrorists are simply evil criminals, enemies of society. They use the kind of thinking that the people who turn terrorist do. Terrorists and those who incite, fund, and train terrorists believe that the leaders of the great powers they threaten are evil criminals, enemies of a just society. Each side feels justified in killing the other. The result is an escalation of hate that produces more terrorism, not less. When a society is sick, the more terrorists one kills, the more people turn terrorist.

Making war for oil or for Allah is not the *cause* of the sickness of the world but its dramatic symptom and tragic consequence. The cause is old thinking—wrong thinking.

Another example of old thinking is the so-called war on poverty, which is fought mainly through financial measures. The negative developments of the past decades are said to be due to a lack of adequate development aid. The rich nations have given aid at an average level of about 0.2 percent of their gross national product (GNP), although they had formally agreed to 0.7 percent of GNP. The current United Nations–endorsed project called the Millennium Development Goals-Based Poverty Reduction Strategy (MDG-based strategy) asks only for 0.5 percent in aid. This would generate $150 billion a year over a period of 20 years. Economist Jeffrey Sachs, special advisor to UN Secretary-General Kofi Annan and the principal author of the strategy, maintains that this could wipe out the extreme poverty now affecting 1.1 billion people by the year 2015.

Sachs presents the MDG-based strategy as an economic and political "global compact," but on a closer look it becomes clear that it involves far more than politics and economics. Achieving the goals of the strategy, as Sachs himself points out, calls for the world to pull together in a unified and coordinated manner, not just to give money, but collectively to fight disease, promote good science and widespread education, provide critical infrastructure, and act in unison in helping the poorest of the poor. Collective action on all these levels, Sachs says, is needed to underpin economic success. Success in the fight against terrorism, as in the war on poverty, calls not just for better security or more money but for new thinking: change in the very texture of the civilization that governs today's world.

The situation is much the same when cities and states fight criminality. They attempt to do so through bigger police forces, more jails, and more rigorous sentences, rather than eliminating the conditions that breed criminality: big city slums, joblessness, and the sense of futility and hopelessness that infects the minds of many people, especially young people. The case is not fundamentally different with regard to fighting environmental degradation either: These problems are *produced by* profit-hungry, ecologically irresponsible practices, and they are *fought by* profit-hungry practices that claim to be ecologically responsible—the latter differ from the former only in making a profit from cleaning up the mess rather than creating it. Winning this particular "fight" also calls for new thinking: recognizing that making a profit and achieving growth are not the sole criteria of success in business; social and environmental responsibility are just as important and are just as much a part of the business of business.

The point need not be belabored. Suffice it to say that in almost all aspects of social and economic activity, and in politics as well as in the private sphere, the mainstream of contemporary society disregards Einstein's warning. It is trying to solve the problems generated by the mindset of industrial civilization with the same materialistic, manipulative, and self-centered rationality that characterizes that mindset.

A change in the thinking that characterizes the fundamental texture of a civilization is not an unprecedented occurrence; it has come about in various epochs in history. In the past, there was time for new thinking to evolve. The rhythm of change was relatively slow; a mindset adapted to the changed conditions had several generations to come about. This is no longer the case. The critical period for new thinking is now compressed into a single lifetime.

In the next few years, new thinking and new action will be crucial; without them, our globalized systems could break down in chaos. A breakdown, however, is our destiny only if we fail to seize the opportunity to choose a better path.

While a global breakdown is already on the radar screen, achieving a global breakthrough remains entirely possible. Seizing this alternative calls for the kind of new thinking that could give birth to a new civilization. This book is dedicated to outlining what that breakthrough is and how we can use it to create a better future for ourselves and our children.

2

The Birthing of a New World

New thinking starts with greater insight into the transformation that ushers in a new world in place of the old. But for new thinking to be effective, we should have some idea of what it involves. Just what kind of a process is the birthing of a new world?

Talk of fundamental change in the world around us is often met with skepticism. Change in society, we are told, is never really fundamental: as the French saying goes, *plus ça change, plus c'est la même chose* (the more things change, the more they are the same). After all, we are dealing with humans and human nature, and these will be very much the same tomorrow as they are today.

A more sophisticated variant of the prevalent view adds that certain processes in society—trends—make a significant difference as they unfold. Trends, whether local or global, micro or mega, introduce a measure of change: As they unfold, there are more of some things and less of others. This is still not fundamental change, for the world is still much the same, only some people are better off and others worse off. This view is the one typically held by futurists, forecasters, business consultants, and all manner of trend analysts. Their extrapolations are highly regarded, as the popularity of literature dealing with megatrends attests.

Governmental agencies also engage in forecasting trends. The unclassified report of the U.S. National Intelligence Council, *Global Trends 2015: A Dialogue about the Future with Nongovernmental Experts,* was published in 2000.

According to this document, the state of the world in the year 2015 will be determined by the unfolding of key trends, catalyzed by key drivers. The seven key trends and drivers are demographics, natural resources and environment, science and technology, the global economy and globalization, national and international governance, future conflict, and the role of the United States. The way these trends unfold under the impact of their drivers can produce four different futures: a future of inclusive globalization, another future of pernicious globalization, a future of regional competition, or a postpolar world. The main deciders are the effects of globalization—positive or negative—and the level and management of the world's potential for interstate and interregional conflict.

When the trends unfold without major disruption, we get what the experts call "the optimistic scenario." In this perspective, the world of 2015 is much like today's world except that some population segments (alas, a shrinking minority) are better off and other segments (a growing majority) are less well-off. The global economy continues to grow, although its path is rocky and marked by financial volatility and a widening economic divide.

Economic growth may be undone, however, by events such as a sustained financial crisis or a prolonged disruption of energy supplies. Other "discontinuities" may occur as well:

- Violent political upheavals due to a serious deterioration of living standards in the Middle East (this has now happened, with dramatic consequences)
- The formation of an international terrorist coalition with anti-Western aims and access to high-tech weaponry (now a real and growing threat)
- Rapidly changing weather patterns that inflict grave damage on human health and on economies (this is now more imminent than ever)
- A global epidemic on the scale of HIV/AIDS
- The antiglobalization movement growing until it becomes a threat to Western governmental and corporate interests
- The emergence of a geostrategic alliance—possibly of Russia, China, and India—aimed at counterbalancing the United States and Western influence
- Collapse of the alliance between the United States and Europe
- Creation of a counterforce organization that could undermine the power of the International Monetary Fund and the World Trade Organization and thus the ability of the United States to exercise global economic leadership

In the year 2000, it was anybody's guess whether the world of 2015 would be the same kind of world or something quite different. In 2010, this is no longer an open question. The world in 2015 will be very different from what it is today—not to mention from what it was at the beginning of this century.

The National Intelligence Council, however, is still producing linear extrapolations on what the future will be like. According to another report published in 2005, titled *Mapping the Global Future* and based on consultations with 1,000 futurists around the globe, the world in 2020 will not be very different from today. Terrorism will still be present, although the prospect of wars conducted by major powers will recede. It is a "relative certainty" that the United States will remain the most powerful nation, economically, technologically, and militarily, although a possible—but manageable—erosion of U.S. power must also be reckoned with.

Such reports highlight the limits of trend-based forecasting. They ignore the fact that trends do not only unfold in time; they can break down and give rise to new trends, new processes, and different conditions. This possibility needs to be considered, since no trend operates in an infinitely adapted environment; its present and future have limits. These may be natural limits due to finite resources and supplies, or human and social limits due to changing structures, values, and expectations. When a major trend encounters such limits, the world is changing and a new dynamic enters into play. Extrapolating existing trends does not help in defining the emerging world.

To know what happens when a trend breaks down calls for deeper insight. It calls for going beyond the observation of current trends and following their expected path—it requires knowing something about the developmental dynamics of the system in which the observed trends appear and may disappear. Such knowledge is provided by modern systems theory, especially the branch popularly known as "chaos theory." Because of the unsustainability of many aspects of today's world, the dynamics of development that will apply to the future is not the linear dynamics of classical extrapolation but the nonlinear chaos dynamics of complex-system evolution.

The Dynamics of Transformation: A Brief Excursion into Chaos Theory

At the dawn of the second decade of the twenty-first century we can no longer ignore that current trends are building toward critical thresholds, toward some of the famous (or infamous) "planetary limits" that in the 1970s and 1980s were said to be the limits to growth. Whether they are limits to growth altogether is questionable, but they are clearly limits to the *kind* of growth that is occurring today. As we move toward these limits, we are approaching a point of chaos. At this point, some trends will deflect or disappear, and new ones will appear in their stead. This is not unusual: Chaos theory shows that the evolution of complex systems always involves alternating periods of stability and instability, continuity and discontinuity, order and chaos. We are living in the opening phases of a period of social and ecological instability—at a crucial decision-window. When we reach the point of chaos, the stable "point" and "periodic" attractors of our systems will be joined by "chaotic" or "strange" attractors. These will appear suddenly, as chaos theorists say, "out of the blue." They will drive our systems to the crucial point where it will select the one or the other of the paths of evolution available to it.

In the current decision-window, our world is supersensitive, so that even small fluctuations produce large-scale effects. These are the legendary "butterfly effects." The story goes that if a monarch butterfly flaps its wings in California, it creates a tiny air fluctuation that amplifies and amplifies and ends by creating a storm over Mongolia.

The discovery of the butterfly effect is linked with the art of weather forecasting, having its roots in the shape assumed by the first chaotic attractor discovered by U.S. meteorologist Edward Lorenz in the 1960s. When Lorenz attempted to computer-model the supersensitive evolution of the world's weather, he found a strange evolutionary path, consisting of two different trajectories joined together like the wings of a butterfly (see page 98 in the postscript). The slightest disturbance would shift the evolutionary trajectory of the world's weather from one wing to the other. The weather, it appears, is a system in a permanently chaotic state—a system permanently governed by chaotic attractors.

Subsequently, a considerable variety of chaotic attractors has been discovered. They are applicable in some measure to all complex systems, above all to living systems. Living systems are remarkable systems; they do not move toward equilibrium, as classical physical systems do, but maintain themselves in their improbable state far from chemical and thermal equilibrium by constantly replenishing the energies and matter they consume with fresh energies and matter flowing from their environment. (Physicists say that they balance the positive entropy they produce internally by importing negative entropy from their surroundings.)

Humans, as other complex organisms, are supersensitive dynamic systems permanently at the edge of chaos, as are the ecologies and societies formed by living systems. These collective systems are wider and more enduring than their individual members, but the dynamics of systems evolution applies also to them.

The evolution of individual and collective organic systems can usually be described with differential equations that map the behavior of the systems in reference to the principal system constraints. This is not feasible in regard to the societies formed by human beings; here the presence of mind and consciousness complicates the evolutionary dynamics. The consciousness of its human members influences the system's behavior, making it far more complex than the behavior of nonhuman systems.

In periods of relative stability, the consciousness of individuals does not play a decisive role in the behavior of society, since a stable social system dampens deviations and isolates the deviants. But when a society reaches the limits of its stability and turns chaotic, it becomes supersensitive, responsive even to small fluctuations such as changes in the values, beliefs, worldviews, and aspirations of its members.

We now live in a period of transformation when a new world is struggling to be born. Ours is an era of decision—a window of unprecedented freedom to decide our destiny. In this decision-window, "fluctuations"—in themselves small and seemingly powerless actions and initiatives—pave the way toward the critical "chaos point" where the system tips in one direction or another. This process is neither predetermined nor random. It is a systemic process that can be purposively steered.

As consumers and clients, as taxpayers and voters, and as public opinion holders we can create the kinds of fluctuations—the actions and initiatives—that will tip the coming chaos point toward peace and sustainability. If we are aware of this power in our hands, and if we have the will and the wisdom to make use of it, we become masters of our destiny.

Chaos Dynamics in Society

The transformation of society is not a chance-ridden haphazard process; chaos and systems theory disclose that it follows a recognizable pattern. Typically the transformation manifests four major phases.

1. The Trigger Phase. Innovations in "hard" technologies (tools, machines, operational systems) bring about greater efficiency in the manipulation of nature for human ends.

2. The Accumulation Phase. Hard technology innovations change social and environmental relations and bring about, successively

• Higher levels of resource production
• Faster growth of population
• Increasing societal complexity
• Increasing impact on the social and the natural environment

3. The Decision-Window. Changed social and environmental relations put pressure on the established order, placing into question time-honored values and worldviews and the ethics and ambitions associated with them. Society becomes unstable, supersensitive to all fluctuations.

4. The Chaos Point. Here the system is critically unstable. The status quo becomes unsustainable and the system's evolution tips in one direction or another:

4a. Evolution ("Devolution") toward Breakdown. The values, worldviews, and ethics of a critical mass of people in society are resistant to change, or change too slowly, and the established institutions are too rigid to allow for timely transformation. Inequity and conflict, coupled with an impoverished environment, create unmanageable stresses. The social order degenerates into conflict and violence.

or

4b. Evolution to Breakthrough. The mindset of a critical mass of people evolves in time, shifting the development of society toward a more adaptable mode. As these changes take hold, the improved order—governed by more adapted values, worldviews, and ethics—establishes itself. The economic, political, and ecological dimensions of society stabilize in a nonconflictual and sustainable mode.

We now look at the four-phase process of societal transformation in the context of the contemporary world.

1. The Trigger Phase, 1800–1960. *Innovations in "hard" technologies (tools, machines, operational systems) trigger fundamental changes in the way people live and work for the sake of creating greater efficiency in organizing people, resources, and nature to reach the desired ends.*

Until the second half of the eighteenth century, the 8,000 years that separated the rise of the Neolithic from the advent of the Industrial Age saw relatively few fundamental technological innovations. Basic agricultural tools were refined but not substantially modified: The sickle, hoe, chisel, saw, hammer, and knife continued in use in substantially unchanged forms. More radical changes occurred only in regard to the technologies of irrigation and the introduction of new varieties of plants.

By the year 1800, the Industrial Revolution had been brewing in England for about half a century. Yet even in the three countries at the forefront of the revolution—England, France, and the United States—there were no telegraph, no railroads, no macadamized roads, no steamboats. The iron and steel industries were still embryonic. But the steamboat was invented in 1802, and oil was found in Pennsylvania in 1859. In the middle of the nineteenth century, the Industrial Revolution entered into full swing, bringing an entire battery of new technologies onto the scene.

The first breakthroughs occurred in textiles: Innovations in spinning cotton stimulated related inventions, leading to machines capable of factory-based mass production. Industrial development soon spread from textiles to iron, as cheaper cast iron replaced more expensive wrought iron.

Closely following on the heels of innovations in the machine tool industry were developments in the chemical industry. Many of the twentieth-century technologies in the automobile, steel, cement, petrochemical, and pharmaceutical industries were spawned in the 1860s and the years that followed. Modern steel mills are for the most part still based on the Bessemer steel process developed at that time; the rotary kiln, patented by Fredrick Rancome in 1885, is still used in today's cement production; and the synthetic dyes of the late eighteenth century were basic to the development of modern chemical industries. The traction-based combustion engine, a key innovation in modern transportation, appeared in the 1880s simultaneously with Edison's electric light bulb, followed by Marconi's wireless and the Wright brothers' flying machine.

In the first half of the twentieth century, these technological innovations shifted industrial production from coal and steam, textiles, machine tools, glass, pre-Bessemer forged steel, and labor-intensive agriculture to electricity, the internal combustion engine, organic chemistry, and large-scale manufacturing.

2. The Accumulation Phase, 1960 to the Present. *Hard technology innovations accumulate and irreversibly transform social and environmental relations. They bring about, at an ever-increasing rate,*

- *Higher levels of resource production*
- *Faster growth in the population*
- *Increasing societal complexity*
- *Increasing impact on the natural environment*

In the early 1960s, nearly 160 years after the innovations that led to the unfolding of the first industrial revolution, a new type of technological innovation occurred. The "second industrial revolution" replaced reliance on massive energy and raw material inputs with the more intangible resource known as *information.* In the last quarter of the twentieth century, a rapidly growing quantity of information came to be stored on optical disks, communicated via fiber optics, with computers equipped with sophisticated programs elaborating the data. The new "soft" technologies made the classical "hard" technologies more efficient. Sophisticated information systems rationalized and dropped the cost of production and consumption and led to vast increments in the mining, production, use, and, ultimately, discard of the manufactured goods produced by ever more powerful automated or semiautomated technologies.

The spread of industrial technologies to the four corners of the globe produced a series of profound transformations, globalizing the economic and financial sectors while leaving social structures locally diverse and disparate. For a minority it brought new wealth and great increases in the material standard of living, but for the growing masses it brought deepening poverty and seemingly hopeless marginalization. Uneven and imbalanced globalization sparked a new gold rush for the wealth promised by the high-technology service and production sectors. The unreflective rush for wealth broke apart traditional structures and placed in question established values and priorities. It led to the exploitation, and occasionally overexploitation, of both renewable and nonrenewable resources, and it degraded the livability of the urban as well as the rural environment.

3. The Window of Decision, 2010–2012 and Beyond. *The dominant social order is stressed by radically changed conditions that place in question established values, worldviews, ethics, and aspirations. Society enters a period of ferment. Now the flexibility and creativity of the people create that subtle but all-important "fluctuation" that decides which of the available paths of development society will hereafter take.*

By the end of the twentieth century, globalization had reached a new phase: The world system had become increasingly and visibly unsustainable. In the first decade of the twenty-first century, the progressive globalization of the economy, coupled with intensifying contact among disparately developed cultures and societies, builds toward a critical epoch in which our systems become unsustainable and increasingly sensitive to change. This state is triggered by high levels of stress, including terrorism and war, conflict in the political sphere, vulnerability in the economic arena, volatility in the financial sphere, and worsening problems with climate and the environment.

4. The Chaos Point, 2012 and the Years that Follow. *The processes initiated at the dawn of the nineteenth century and accelerating since the 1960s build inevitably toward a decision-window and then toward a critical threshold of no return: the chaos point. Now a simple rule holds: We cannot stand still, we cannot go back, we must keep moving. There are alternative ways we can move forward. There is a path to breakdown, as well as a path to a new world.*

In remarkable—and *perhaps* not entirely fortuitous agreement with the date predicted by the Mayan civilization, the Chaos Point is likely to be reached on or just beyond the year 2012. The Mayan calendar indicates that the "Age of Jaguar," the thirteenth *baktun,* or long period of 144,000 days, will come to an end with the fifth and final Sun on December 22, 2012. That date, according to the Mayan system, will mark the "gateway" to a new epoch of planetary development, with a radically different kind of consciousness.

The year 2012 is indeed likely to be a gateway to a different world, but whether to a better world or to a disastrous one is yet to be decided. At that point, alternative paths open to us:

(a) The Breakdown Path: Devolution to Disaster

Rigidity and lack of foresight lead to stresses that the established institutions can no longer contain. Conflict and violence assume global proportions, and anarchy follows in their wake.

or

(b) The Breakthrough Path: Evolution to a New Civilization

A new way of thinking with more adapted values and more evolved consciousness mobilizes people's will and catalyzes a fresh surge of creativity. People and institutions master the stresses that arose in the wake of the preceding generation's unreflective fascination with technology and untrammeled pursuit of wealth and power. By the year 2032, a new era dawns for humanity.

The insight we get from this four-phase transformation dynamic is simple and straightforward. In society, fundamental change is triggered by technological innovations that destabilize the established structures and institutions. More adapted structures and institutions await the surfacing of a more adapted mindset in the bulk of the population. Thus in the transformation of our world, technological innovation is the trigger. The decider, however, is not more technology, but the rise of new thinking—new values, perceptions, and priorities—in a critical mass of the people who make up the bulk of society.

3

The Drivers of Chaos

The choice we presently face is between devolution toward crisis and breakdown, and evolution toward a new world. We will enter one or the other path, for the world as it is today is not sustainable. Let us look now at the factors that drive us toward this crucial crossroads.

The Economic Unsustainabilities

The first driver: The unsustainability of the current distribution of wealth in the world. Economic growth continues in the world, but it is both precarious and unfair. Its benefits regard ever fewer people and marginalize ever more. Hundreds of millions live at a higher material standard of living, but thousands of millions are pressed into abject poverty, living in shantytowns and urban ghettos in the shadows of ostentatious affluence. The richest 20 percent earn 90 times the income of the poorest 20 percent, consume 11 times as much energy, eat 11 times as much meat, have 49 times the number of telephones, and own 145 times the number of cars. The net worth of 500 billionaires equals the net worth of half the world population. This is not only unjust and indefensible—it is highly explosive.

The absolute deprivation of over one billion people and the relative poverty of two-thirds of the world's population is an arbitrary condition; one cannot ascribe the blame for it to a finite planet. If access to the Earth's physical and biological resources were evenly distributed, all people in the world could live at a decent material standard. For example, if food supplies were equitably shared, every person would receive about a hundred calories more than are required to replace the 1,800 to 3,000 calories he or she expends each day (a healthy diet calls for an intake of about 2,600 calories). But people in the rich countries of North America, Western Europe, and Japan obtain not 100 percent, but 140 percent of their 2,600 caloric requirement, whereas people in the poorest countries, such as Madagascar, Guyana, and Laos, are limited to 70 percent. Americans spend only 10 percent of their income on food, and still buy so much that they throw away 15 percent of it. Haitians, some 600 miles to the south, as well as three-fourths of all Africans, spend more than half their income on food and are undernourished. This is a structural problem. Surveys by the UN Development Programme and the Food and Agriculture Organization indicate that 87 countries today neither produce sufficient food to sustain their population nor have the money to import the missing amount from elsewhere.

The world's pattern of energy consumption is just as disparate. The average amount of commercial electrical energy consumed by Africans is half a kilowatt-hour (kWh) per person. The corresponding average for Asians and Latin Americans is 2 to 3 kWh; and Americans, Europeans, Australians, and Japanese use up to 8 kWh. With 4.1 percent of the world population, the United States alone consumes 25 percent of the world's energy production, much of it wastefully—for example, by heating homes with inefficient gas-powered heaters or electric radiators in the winter, leaving air conditioners on for extended periods in the summer, and using gas-guzzling vans, pickup trucks, and sport utility vehicles for everyday transportation. The average American burns five tons of fossil fuel per year—in contrast with the 0.8 tons of the average Chinese and the still somewhat modest 2.9 tons of the average German.

In the course of the 80-plus years of expected life span of a child born to a middle-class family in the United States, he or she will consume 800,000 kilowatts of electrical energy. In addition, he or she will also consume 2,500,000 liters of water; 21,000 tons of gasoline; 220,000 kilos of steel; the wood of 1,000 trees, and will generate 60 tons of municipal waste. At these rates, the average American child will produce in his or her lifetime twice the environmental load of a Swedish child, three times that of an Italian, 13 times that of a Brazilian, 35 times that of an Indian, and 280 times that of a Haitian.

The second driver: The unsustainability of affluent consumption. Even if global economic growth were to continue beyond the next few years (which, as we shall see, is questionable), it would likely be highly concentrated, accruing mainly to rich countries, rich corporations, and persons in positions of power. Even on a global growth-scenario, by the middle of the twenty-first century some 90 percent of the world's people would live in the poor countries, and the great majority of them would be themselves poor. If today's highly unequal distribution of wealth is not rectified, it is difficult to see how they could satisfy even their most basic needs. As Gandhi said, although the world has enough to provide for all people's *need,* it does not have enough to cater to even one person's *greed.*

In the rich countries of the world, greed is still dominant. In the name of the free market, many people use not only what they need, but all they can get. Affluent people use 80 percent of the world's energy and raw materials and contribute the lion's share of its pollution. The average human needs five liters of water a day for drinking and cooking and 25 liters for personal hygiene, but the average American uses 350 liters a day—80 liters just for flushing the toilet—and the average European and Japanese, 130 to 150 liters. At the same time, many Africans walk two miles to get safe water, if indeed they can get any; 48 percent of them lack access to water that is safe for drinking and cooking.

Greed is also evident in the way people eat. The average Englishman each month consumes six bags of chips, six chocolate bars, six bags of candy, three sandwiches, two pies, two burgers, a donut, and a kebab while sitting behind the wheel. On an annual basis, Americans, worried about obesity, spend 30 times more trying to slim down than the UN's entire budget for famine relief. Affluent people consume such quantities of red meat that the world's entire grain harvest would not be enough to feed all the cattle that would be needed if the poorer people of the world were to adopt a similar diet. Yet poor people are attempting to do just that: Meat consumption in the developing countries has tripled between 1980 and 2004, going from fifty to 150 million tons. And, according to the Food and Agriculture Organization (FAO), it is expected to increase by another 110 million tons by 2030.

Affluent consumption is not the only cause of the unsustainability of the modern world; the way poor people attempt to obtain the resources required for their survival is a problem as well. The 1.1 billion people who, according to World Bank estimates, live at or below the absolute poverty line (defined as the equivalent of one dollar a day or less) destroy the environment on which they depend. Whether in the cities or in the countryside, poverty makes for the overworking of productive lands, the contamination of rivers and lakes, and the lowering of water tables. This creates a vicious cycle. Poverty encourages high birthrates, because children help subsistence families garner the resources needed for survival. Population growth creates more poverty, and more poor people destroy more of the environment.

With rural environments degrading, people abandon their native towns and villages and flee to the cities. Urban complexes have experienced explosive growth: One out of every three people now lives in a city, and by the year 2025 two out of every three are expected to do so. By that year, there will be more than 500 cities with populations of over one million, and 30 megacities exceeding eight million. Such cities are intrinsically unsustainable. The bigger they are, the greater their dependence on their already overexploited environment.

Well-to-do people overuse the planet's resources, and poor people misuse them. Of the nearly seven billion people on the planet, the two billion "developed" consume and waste more than their share, while the three billion "underdeveloped" misuse what little is left to them. To make things worse, many of the two billion in the middle, the "developing" masses, hope to adopt the life ways and consumption patterns of the two billion "developed." But this ambition is more than the resources and ecosystems of the planet can fulfill.

A particularly striking example is the consumption curve in China. Overall, the consumption of grain and meat as well as of coal and steel is higher today in China than in the United States. It cannot keep growing without disastrous consequences for the planet. According to calculations by the Earth Policy Institute, if China's consumption were to rise to the American level on a per-person basis, the demand would be more than the earth's resources could fulfill. For example, if Chinese people were to consume the 935 kilograms of meat per person that Americans consume annually (the Chinese now consume 291 kilograms), by 2031 they would require two-thirds of the current world grain production (181 million tons) to feed their herds. If they were to burn coal at the present U.S. level, they would use more coal in a single year than today's entire annual coal production. And if Chinese people were to use oil at the same rate as Americans now do, they would use more oil than the world is ever likely to produce: 2.8 billion tons a year, compared with the current world production, which has already peaked at 2.5 billion.

In China, as throughout the developing world, the lifestyles of the affluent are admired and emulated. Because the two billion "developed" drive a private car to work, shopping, and recreation—even in cities where public transport is available—the two billion "developing" hope to own and use cars for much the same reasons and the same purposes. A good portion of the 1.3 billion Chinese are on the way to realizing this ambition. In the center of the "miracle city" Shenzhen, there are hardly any bicycles left, but private cars, including luxury models, abound— together with traffic jams and air pollution. Much the same emulation occurs in regard to eating habits. Because people in the industrialized countries have a preference for steaks and hamburgers, people in China and other developing countries aspire to the same kind of diet. Hamburger stands and fast-food restaurants are springing up throughout the poor countries and regions of the South. Even Eskimos in the North drink Coke and eat hamburgers.

Suppose, then, that the two billion "developed" decided to live in a more responsible way. Would that make a difference to the aspirations of the two billion hopefully "developing," and the condition of the three billion almost hopelessly "underdeveloped"? It very likely would. Simpler lifestyles and more responsible choices would free a significant portion of the planet's resources for consumption by all the people who inhabit it. It takes the yield of 190 square meters of land and no less than 105,000 liters of water to produce one kilogram of grain-fed feedlot beef. But to produce one kilogram of soybeans takes only 16 square meters of land and 9,000 liters of water. The same amount of land that produces one kilogram of beef could produce nearly 12 kilograms of soybeans or 8.6 kilograms of corn. And the farmers would save 96,000 liters of water by choosing soybeans and 92,500 liters by planting corn. Given the rapid erosion of many agricultural lands and the coming water squeeze, this difference may be crucial.

The Fallacies of Overconsumption:
The Cases of Eating, Smoking, and Driving

World meat consumption has increased more than fivefold in the last 50 years. More and more people demand meat, yet the meat they get is not the safe meat one's grandmother bought in 1950. It may contain progesterone, testosterone, avoparcin, and clenbuterol—chemicals farmers pump into cattle to fatten them up and keep them healthy. Anabolic steroids, growth hormones, and beta-agonists turn fat into muscle; antibiotics stimulate growth and protect sedentary animals against diseases they would not get if they were kept in more natural conditions.

A diet heavy on meat is not only unhealthy, it is also immoral: It indulges a personal fancy at the expense of depleting resources essential to feed the entire human population. Red meat comes from cattle, and cattle must be fed. The grain fed to cattle is subtracted from that available for human consumption. If cows returned equivalent nutrition in the form of meat, their feed would not be wasted. But the calorific energy provided by beef is only one-seventh of the energy of the feed. This means that in the process of converting grain into beef, cows "waste" six-sevenths of the nutritional value of their feed. The proportion is somewhat more favorable in poultry, but the average chicken still uses for itself two-thirds of the nutritional value of the feed it consumes.

It is true that land too poor for crops can be used to graze livestock. Nonetheless, there is not enough grain to feed the animals that would be needed to supply meat for the tables of all the people in the world. The giant herds of cattle and endless farms of poultry would require more grain than the total output of the planet's agricultural lands—according to some calculations, about twice as much. Given the amount of land available for farming and the known and presently used agricultural methods, doubling today's grain production would call for economically prohibitive investments. The rational and moral solution is to phase out the mass production of cattle and poultry—not by massive slaughter but by breeding fewer animals and breeding them healthier.

The nutritive needs of the entire human population could be satisfied by eating more vegetables and grain and less meat, using first and foremost the produce of one's own country, region, and environment. Grain- and plant-based food self-reliance provides a healthier diet, and it allows the world's economically exploitable agricultural lands to be worked to satisfy the needs of the whole human family.

What goes for meat eating also goes for smoking. The fact that smoking is dangerous to one's own health and the health of others can be read on every packet of cigarettes, but it is not generally known that growing tobacco for export robs millions of poor people of fertile land on which they could grow cereals and vegetables. As long as there is a market for tobacco exports, agribusinesses and profit-hungry farmers will plant tobacco instead of wheat, corn, or soy. And the market for tobacco exports will remain attractive as long as large numbers of people continue to smoke. Tobacco, together with other cash crops such as coffee and tea, commands a considerable portion of the world's fertile lands, yet such produce does not respond to a real necessity.

Reducing the demand for tobacco—and for coffee, tea, and similar cash crops (not to mention opium, heroin, and other psychedelic plants)— would mean a healthier life for all who can afford them (or are hooked on them) and at the same time a chance for adequate nourishment for the poor. A better pattern of land use would permit feeding eight or even ten billion people without conquering new land and engaging in risky experiments with genetically manipulated crop varieties. But with today's consumption patterns, the world's agricultural lands can barely feed the 6.5 billion people living today. It takes only one acre of productive land to provide the average Indian's agriculture-related needs, but satisfying the needs of a typical American takes fully 12 acres. Making 12 acres of productive land available to provide food for 6.5 billion people would require two more planets the size of Earth.

We should also consider the use—or overuse—of the private automobile. Unless there is a rapid shift to new fuel technologies—possible, but difficult to achieve worldwide—doubling the current motor vehicle pool will double the level of smog precursors and greenhouse gases. Cars and trucks will choke the streets of third-world cities and the transportation arteries of developing regions. But the current form and level of motor vehicle use are not necessities in either the industrialized or the developing world. For goods transport, rails and rivers could be more effectively used, and for city dwellers public transportation could be pressed into wide-scale service, reducing the number of private vehicles.

We know that the urban sprawl created by the widespread use of private automobiles is undesirable, that traffic jams are frustrating and counterproductive, and that the gasoline-powered internal combustion engine uses up finite resources and contributes to air pollution and global warming. We also know that there are perfectly good alternatives to the standard automobile: cars running on natural gas or liquid hydrogen, to mention two. Even though these technologies are becoming more widely known, and more of the technologies for their economic production are being developed, the bulk of the consumer population still demands conventionally powered cars. As long as the demand keeps up, industries will not introduce the available alternative technologies, and cities and states will not create cleaner and more efficient public transportation systems.

The third driver: The unsustainability of current developments in the global financial system. At a superficial level, the unsustainability of the global financial system is not apparent. Since the global financial crisis of 2008, the greed and unethical behavior of much of the financial sector has become painfully apparent. And following the crisis of te European monetary system in the spring of 2010, the instability of the current financial sysems has also become clear to everyone. It is becoming painfully evident that the patterns of growth of the last several decades concentrated in China, and a few other Asian economies—are not sustainable. They seriously unbalance the international financial system. In simplest terms, the U.S. consumes too much and exports too little, while China and other Asian countries consume too little and export too much. As a result, the U.S. has a growing trade deficit: the value of the goods it imports is far above the value of the goods it exports. The opposite is the case in China and other Asian economies: they have a growing trade surplus, since the value of their exports is above the value of their imports. The current account deficit of the U.S. (the broadest measure of US trade in goods and services and income and transfer payments) rose from roughly zero to 6.5 percent of US GDP, with about 40 percent of the increase occurring after 2001. The 2008–09 global economic crisis and recession have reduced the deficit—via a sharp decline in oil prices, slow growth, and falling imports—for the near term, but these gains are likely to be short-lived. In 2010 the Peter G. Petersen Institute for International Economics reported that once the economy is back on a steady growth path, the current account deficit will at best return to about 4 percent of GDP, eventually testing the limits of external debt sustainability. But, the economists point out, if the post-recession, long-term US fiscal deficit skyrockets, to 10 percent of GDP instead of adjusting to 2 percent, the current account deficit and foreign debt could explode. By 2030 the current account deficit would soar to more than $5 trillion annually, or more than 15 percent of U.S. GDP. As a result, the net foreign debt of the United States would rise to $50 trillion, or more than 140 percent of GDP, far above any conceivably sustainable positions.

U.S. dollars are a valued currency: more than two-thirds of global reserves are held in dollars. Thus, for now the debt chalked up by the U.S. can be financed by further borrowing in dollars. Central banks with large foreign exchange reserves, like China, Japan, and other Asian countries, remain captives of U.S. fiscal policy. They recognize that refusing further accumulation—let alone reducing their dollar holdings—would push the dollar down, causing large losses on their reserves. In addition, a dollar with smaller buying power would reduce their exports to the U.S., and this would produce unemployment and could threaten recession. These are unwelcome prospects. But how long will the world finance U.S. overspending? The financial imbalance is growing, and it is only a question of time before it will reach a point where it will have to be corrected.

The central bankers know that the alternative to a gradual if painful adjustment is the radical step of switching to another reserve currency. If they do, the U.S. would no longer be able to finance its deficit in dollars, and the American economy would face a shock similar to that which led to the collapse of the Argentine economy. This would have worldwide repercussions.

The IMF's 2005 *Economic Outlook* noted that it is no longer a question whether the world economy will adjust, only *how* it will adjust. If measures required for a gradual adjustment are delayed, the adjustment will be "abrupt." It will be a part, or perhaps a trigger, of the Chaos Point faced by the entire world economy.

The Social Unsustainabilities

The fourth driver: The unsustainability of established social structures. Stresses within human communities are nearing a critical point: Traditional social structures are breaking down. This is partially, but not entirely, the consequence of the explosive growth of population. World population in the year 1900 was about 1.5 billion people. In 2010, it was nearly 7 billion—a well overfourfold increase in just over 100 years. Population is still increasing at the rate of 90 million people annually. United Nations medium-range forecasts speak of 7.85 billion humans by 2025 and 9.1 billion by 2050.

About 98 percent of world population growth is expected to occur in the developing countries. Unless starvation and inhuman living conditions decimate the populations, the centers of poverty will expand radically: The population of the least-developed countries will increase from 800 million today to 1.7 billion in 2050, with population tripling in Afghanistan, Burkina Faso, Burundi, Chad, Congo, East Timor, Guinea-Bissau, Liberia, Mali, Niger, and Uganda.

On the other hand, the population of the industrialized countries will either shrink or at the most remain constant. By mid-century, fertility rates in Japan, Russia, India, Germany, and Italy are expected to be no higher than three-fourths of the level required for maintaining the existing population. In the industrialized world as a whole, the median age will increase from 26 to 37 and the average life expectancy from 65 to 75 years. More people will be 60 or older than will be 15 or younger.

The unsustainability of social conditions in today's world cannot, however, be entirely ascribed to imbalanced patterns of population growth. Family structures are coming apart. In industrialized countries, to raise children in a nurturing environment is becoming more difficult; the rate for first marriages ending in divorce in the United States is 50 percent, and about 40 percent of children grow up in single-parent families for at least part of their childhood. A growing number of men and women find more satisfaction and companionship at work than at home. After children have "flown the nest," it is becoming usual for couples to seek fulfillment with other partners rather than restructuring the family relationship in a childless home.

In all parts of the world, families eat meals together less and less frequently, and when they do, the TV is likely to be the center of attention. Children's media exposure to TV, video games, and "adult" themes—a euphemism for violent and sexually provocative fare—is increasing. Exposure to such imagery, researchers find, connects with violent and sexually exploitive behavior. Teens face the peer challenge of "freer" sex, where loose "hooking up" for one-night stands is coming to be seen as normal, and building deep emotional relationships with sexual partners is considered out of date.

Many of the functions of family life are taken over by outside interest groups. Child rearing is increasingly entrusted to kindergartens and company or community day-care centers. Leisure-time activities are dominated by the results of the marketing and public-relations efforts of commercial enterprises, and the provision of daily nourishment is shifting from the family kitchen to supermarkets, prepared food industries, and fast-food chains.

In developing countries, the exigencies of economic survival are destroying the traditional extended family. As women are obliged to leave the home in search of work, poverty breaks apart even the nuclear family. Women are extensively exploited, given menial jobs for low pay. Children fare even worse. According to the International Labour Office, today 50 million children worldwide (mostly in Africa, Asia, and Latin America) are working. They are employed for a pittance in factories, mines, and on the land, and many are forced to venture into the hazards of life on the street as "self-employed vendors" or just plain beggars.

An even more deplorable consequence of family poverty is the letting go, and sometimes the outright selling, of children into prostitution. UNICEF names this "one of the most abusive, exploitative and hazardous forms of child labor." In Asia alone, one million children are believed to work as juvenile prostitutes, exploited by the highly profitable pedophilia industry, serviced by international sex-tourism.

The Ecological Unsustainabilities

The fifth driver: the unsustainability of the human load on nature. Unsustainable relations have also evolved between human societies and nature. This is a consequence of two basic trends:

- The rapidly growing *demand* for the planet's physical resources and biological wealth

- The accelerating *depletion* of the planet's physical resources and biological wealth

As a result, the rising curve of demand is now crossing the descending curve
of supply. Humankind has consumed more of the Earth's resources in the 60 years
since World War II than in all of history prior to that time. The production of oil,
fish, lumber, and other major resources has already peaked. Half the world's forests
and 25 percent of the coral reefs are now gone, and about 9.4 million hectares of
forest are lost annually.

The continued growth of the population, coupled with the exploitation of the
planet's natural resources, leaves the basic needs of ever more people unsatisfied. This
is an unprecedented situation. For most of our five-million-year history, humankind's
demand has been insignificant in relation to the available resources; with primitive
technologies and smaller populations, planetary resources seemed limitless. Even
when the technologies employed exhausted a local environment and depleted local
resources, there were always other resources and environments to exploit. But in the
last 50 years, the human family has grown more than in all of previous history.

Imbalanced population growth is a problem, but it no more accounts for the
unsustainability of human relations to the biosphere than it accounts for the unsustainability of relations between people. Today's nearly 7 billion humans are less than
0.5 percent of the biomass of animals. Such a small fragment should not be a threat
to the whole biosphere. Yet humanity *is* an acute threat; its impact is entirely out
of proportion to its size.

Numerous international organizations have documented the massive environmental damage caused by the intensive consumption of fossil fuels, agricultural
products, forest products, fresh water supplies, and countless other natural
resources. The "consume and dispose" engine that drives this consumption is a
complex enterprise, the elements of which include subsidies for extraction and
harvesting of metals, timber, and other virgin materials; advertising that equates
self-worth with ownership of goods; and land-use policies that promote materials-
intensive urban sprawl.

Quantitative indices have been developed to calculate the level of humanity's
impact on nature. One such index is the ecological footprint: the area of land
required to support a human community. If the footprint of a settlement is larger
than the area of that settlement, the settlement is not independently sustainable.
Cities are intrinsically unsustainable, because few of the natural resources used by

their inhabitants come from within their borders; most come from hinterlands and catchments in regard to food, water, and other resources. Cities also depend on hinterlands for the disposal of wastes. But entire regions and countries could well be sustainable—their ecological footprint need not extend beyond their boundaries.

A pathbreaking survey commissioned by the Earth Council of Costa Rica examined the ecological footprints of 52 countries; 42 of them had footprints that exceeded their territory.

The optimum sustainable level of agricultural resource production—where the loss of topsoil is reduced and ultimately halted—is 1.7 hectares (4.2 acres). But the average per capita footprint of the countries examined came to 2.8 hectares (6.9 acres). If this average load were reached by the more than 190 countries of the world, the ecological footprint of the human population would be larger than the whole of the biosphere. The only reason this is not the case today is because people in the poor countries have footprints of far less than 1.7 hectares—half a hectare (little more than one acre) per person in Bangladesh, for example, contrasting with 10.3 hectares (25 acres) in the United States.

The unsustainability of the human load on nature is aggravated by the progressive impairment of ecological balances, a degenerative process that was not generally recognized until Rachel Carson published her pathbreaking book *The Silent Spring* in 1962. Yet the life-supporting environment has become dangerously degraded. Chemically bolstered mechanized agriculture increases the yield per acre and makes more acres available for cultivation, but it also increases the growth of algae that chokes lakes and waterways. Chemicals such as DDT are effective insecticides, but they poison entire animal, bird, and insect populations.

Robert Muller, who spent more than 40 years at the United Nations, much of it in the cabinet of the secretary-general, warned that each minute 21 hectares (52 acres) of tropical forest are lost, 50 tons of fertile topsoil are blown off, and 12,000 tons of carbon dioxide are added to the atmosphere, mainly as 35,725 barrels of oil are burned as industrial and commercial fuel. Each hour 685 hectares (1,693 acres) of productive dryland become desert, and each day 250,000 tons of sulfuric acid fall as acid rain in the northern hemisphere.

Waste disposal contributes to the nature-impairment process. We discard much more than our household wastes into the environment. We inject an estimated 100,000 chemical compounds into the land, rivers, and seas; dump millions of tons of sludge and solid waste into the oceans; release billions of tons of

CO_2 into the air; and increase the level of radioactivity in water, land, and air. The wastes discarded into the environment do not vanish; they come back to plague those who produce them as well as other communities near and far. Refuse dumped into the sea returns to poison marine life and infest coastal regions. The smoke rising from homesteads and factories does not dissolve and disappear: The CO_2 released remains in the atmosphere, affecting the world's weather. In the rich countries, vast quantities of chemicals produced by industry are bubbling through the groundwater systems; in poor countries, rivers and lakes have up to a hundred times the accepted level of pollutants. Until recently, the water in Malaysia's Klang River had enough mercury to function as a pesticide.

There has been a massive increase in allergies in both urban and rural environments. The appellations of toxic environmental effects constitute a whole new vocabulary: There is MCS (multiple chemical sensitivity), wood preservative syndrome, solvent intolerance, chemically associated immune dysfunction, clinical ecology syndrome, chronic fatigue syndrome, fibromyalgia, and sick building syndrome, among others.

Landmarks in the Degradation of Nature

Water, air, and soil are both overused and misused, and can no longer regenerate sufficiently to meet the demands of a growing population. Statistics from UNESCO, FAO (the Food and Agricultural Organization), and other UN and world bodies show the details with striking clarity.

Water

Four-fifths of the planet's surface is water, and the idea that humanity could run out of water seems preposterous. But water for human use has to be fresh, and the saltwater in the oceans and seas makes up 97.5 percent of the planet's total water volume. Two-thirds of the remaining water is concentrated in polar icecaps and underground. The renewable freshwater potentially available for human consumption—water in lakes, rivers, and reservoirs—is no more than 0.007 percent of the water on the surface of the Earth. This relatively thin trickle is essential: A person can survive for about a month without food but no more than a week without water.

In the past, the available water reserves were more than enough to satisfy human needs. Even in 1950, there was a potential world reserve of nearly 17,000 m^3 of freshwater for every woman, man, and child. But the rate of water withdrawal has been more than double the rate of population growth, so in 1999 this reserve amount decreased to 7,300 m^3. If current trends continue, in the year 2025 there will be only 4,800 m³ of reserves per person. This would create serious water shortages in many parts of the world.

Just 50 years ago, not a country in the world faced catastrophic water shortages. Today about one-third of the world's population lives under nearly catastrophic conditions, and by 2025 two-thirds of the population will have to cope with such shortages. Europe and the United States will have half the per capita reserves they had in 1950, and Asia and Latin America will have but a quarter. The worst-hit countries will be in Africa, the Middle East, and south and central Asia. Here the available supplies may drop to less than 1,700 m³ per person.

Soil

With the exception of sandy deserts and high mountains, the surface of the continents is covered with soil, but soil of a quality suitable for agriculture is relatively scarce. The UN's Food and Agriculture Organization estimates that there are 3,031 million hectares (about 7,490 million acres) of high-quality cropland now available, 71 percent of which is in the developing world. This is a precious resource, desperately needed to supply the food and agricultural needs of a growing human population. Yet pressures of human activity produce soil erosion, destructuring, compaction, impoverishment, excessive desiccation, accumulation of toxic salts, leaching of nutritious elements, and inorganic and organic pollution due to urban and industrial wastes.

Soil degradation feeds on itself: As scientists at England's Cranfield University discovered, soils in the UK are losing the carbon they contain at an accelerated rate. As temperatures rise, the decomposition of organic matter speeds up, and this causes more warming and hence more decomposition. Lands degraded to desert-like conditions reduce the world's food and agricultural production for centuries; it takes nature 100 to 400 years to create ten millimeters of productive topsoil. To build a topsoil layer of 30 centimeters takes anywhere from 3,000 to 12,000 years. In his authoritative *World Agriculture and Environment*, Jason Clay noted, "There is a steady increase in the consumption of food and fiber produced by agriculture, while at the same time there is a steady decline in the quality and productivity of soil around the world. The two trends are on a collision course."

In some parts of the world, the scarcity and degradation of topsoil augurs major food shortages. China, for example, has a population that is five times that of the United States, but has only one-tenth as much cultivated land. It is feeding 24 percent of the world's population on 7 percent of the world's agricultural land. China manages this feat by employing an enormous agricultural labor force—estimated at 40 percent of the world total—and pumping vast quantities of chemical fertilizers and other chemicals into the soil. This has serious consequences. Of China's 100 million hectares of cultivated land, one-tenth are highly polluted, one-third are suffering from water loss and soil erosion, one-fifteenth are salinized, and nearly 4 percent are in the process of turning into a desert. Due to urban sprawl and the construction of roads and factories, 15 million hectares of China's cultivated land have been turned to nonagricultural use—an area equal to the agricultural lands of France and Italy combined.

Worldwide, humanity is losing five to seven million hectares of cropland per year. If this process continues, some 300 million hectares will be lost by mid-century, leaving 2.7 billion hectares to support over nine billion people. This would yield an average of 0.3 hectares (or 0.74 acres) per person, the subsistence level of food production for the entire human population.

Air

At first, the idea that we could overexploit the atmosphere that surrounds the planet seems unlikely. After all, this is an envelope some 20 kilometers deep, spread evenly from the polar icecaps to the tropical equator. The amount of air that humans, or even all living organisms taken together, need is minuscule compared to this vast supply. But, as with water, it is not a question of how much we need, but in what form we need it. It is a question of quality rather than quantity. Salty or polluted water is not of much use when it comes to ensuring the survival of the human population, and polluted air of poor quality is also of little use. Yet we are changing the composition of the planet's atmosphere. We are reducing its oxygen content and increasing its carbon dioxide and other greenhouse gas content.

Evidence from prehistoric times indicates an oxygen content of the atmosphere well above today's 21 percent of total volume. Oxygen in the air has decreased in recent times mainly due to the burning of coal, which began in the middle of the nineteenth century. The oxygen content of the atmosphere now dips to 19 percent over impacted areas and is down to 12 to 17 percent over major cities. This level is insufficient to keep body cells, organs, and the immune system functioning at full efficiency; cancers and other degenerative diseases are likely to develop. At oxygen levels of six or seven percent of the volume of air, life can no longer be sustained.

The human impact on the atmosphere has reduced the atmosphere's oxygen content and has increased the share of other elements. The increase in atmospheric greenhouse gases such as carbon dioxide is particularly important. Two hundred years of burning fossil fuels and cutting down large tracts of forest have increased the atmosphere's carbon dioxide content from about 280 parts per million to more than 350 parts per million.

The influx of gases from human activity is paralleled by the growing influx of gases from nature, and this influx is now largely due to human activity. In Siberia, an area of permafrost spanning a million square kilometers, the size of France and Germany combined, has started to melt for the first time since it formed at the end of the last ice age 11,000 years ago. Russian researchers found that what was until recently a barren expanse of frozen peat is turning into a broken landscape of mud and lakes, some more than a kilometer across. The area, the world's largest frozen peat bog, has been producing methane since it formed at the end of the last ice age, but most of the gas has been trapped under the permafrost.

The west Siberian peat bog may hold as much as 70 billion tons of methane, a quarter of all of the methane stored in the ground around the world. Calculations show that the melting peat bog could release around 700 million tons of carbon into the atmosphere each year, about the same amount that is released annually from all of the world's wetlands and agriculture. This would double atmospheric levels of the gas, leading to a ten percent to 25 percent increase in global warming.

The Climate

Changes in the chemical composition of the atmosphere trigger alterations in the climate. Climate change has already reached the danger point. A report published in 2005 by the Institute for Public Policy Research in the United Kingdom, the Center for American Progress in the United States, and the Australia Institute specified the point of no return: the Chaos Point beyond which global temperature change has massively disastrous consequences. This is a rise in the average global temperature two degrees Celsius above the average in the year 1750. This may seem a small change to produce such vast consequences, but climate models indicate that it could produce widespread harvest failures, water shortages, increased spread of diseases, the rise of the sea level, and the die-out of major forests.

Global temperatures have now risen 0.8 degrees Celsius, and the warming trend is accelerating. Temperatures in the western Arctic are at a 400-year high; and in September of 2005, satellite pictures testified that the extent of the Arctic ice-cap was 20 percent below the long-term average for the month of September. If this trend continues, the Arctic Ocean will be completely ice-free well before the end of the century. This is a realistic prospect, since the warming process feeds on itself: as ice disappears, the surface of the sea becomes darker, absorbing more heat. Less ice forms, which means that the sea becomes still darker, absorbing still more heat.

The progressive reduction of the Arctic ice-cap alters the world's weather. It threatens first of all Europe, as the volume of freshwater streaming into the North Atlantic would end by deflecting the Gulf Stream. That would flood Western Europe with frigid waters, creating winters of Siberian cold over England and much of the continent.

While Europe is threatened with a colder climate, most of the planet is subjected to rising temperatures. If nothing decisive is done to deflect the warming trend, the damage to the Amazon rainforest, already apparent, will become irreversible. There will be widespread destruction of coral reefs, the alpine flora of Europe and Australia will disappear, and there will be severe losses of China's broad-leaved forests.

The climate change triggered by higher temperatures will play havoc with the production of agricultural lands. Although in cold regions with short growing seasons it could increase yields, it will decrease harvests in tropical and subtropical areas where crops are already growing near the limit of their heat tolerance. These effects are not precisely foreseeable: Global warming is not a gradual and distributed process but a differential warming and cooling effect over different parts of the globe. But in their totality, these alterations in the climate threaten untold living species. They are also a threat to the food supply and, hence, to the very survival of human communities the world over.

4

Parameters of a Positive Transformation

The data we have just reviewed tells us that we are approaching a critical condition: Our world has become economically, socially, and ecologically unsustainable. Persisting in the values and practices of the rationalistic, manipulative civilization of the modern world will create deepening rifts between rich and poor, young and old, informed and marginalized, and could make the biosphere inhospitable for most of humanity. To survive in our planetary home, we must create a world better adapted to the conditions we have ourselves created.

Can we create a more adapted world? This question can be more precisely stated. Can the power- and wealth-oriented civilization of the Industrial Age be effectively and sufficiently transformed to ensure the survival and well-being of the entire human population? Civilizations are not eternal; they are subject to change, even to fundamental transformation. Past civilizations have transformed throughout history; could ours transform as well?

Transformations in History

In their classic textbook *Civilization Past and Present* historians of civilization Walter Wallbank and Alastair Taylor noted that ever since our forebears evolved some form of culture and some form of social order, periodic shifts in the relations to each other and to nature were accompanied by corresponding shifts in their thinking. Together, these "objective" and "subjective" shifts produced total-system transformations—shifts in civilization. Before looking at the feasibility of a positive transformation of our own civilization we should review the major transformations of civilization in the past. They may hold important lessons for the transformation we face today.

Transformation from Mythos to Theos

About a million years ago, the earliest bands of five to 80 nomads, consisting of one or more extended families, spread from Africa into Eurasia. These Paleolithic people held territory in common and had an informal leadership based on personality, strength, and fighting skills. Everyone, including children, foraged for food, and adult males engaged in hunting. The technologies they used were simple but effective. They consisted of objects improvised as tools or as weapons, and later of the purposive fashioning of objects (such as hand axes) according to tradition. These served for hunting and warfare, for making and controlling fire, for adapting and building shelters, and for rites and rituals connected with birth, maturity, and death.

By 11,000 B.C.E. in the Fertile Crescent, the formerly verdant region extending from the Levant to Persia (now Iran), human groups had grown into tribes of several hundred living in fixed settlements. This was made possible by the concentration of resources such as wild cereals. In the larger and more complex human groups of this Neolithic Age, additional technologies came into use, including cultivating plants, husbanding animals, and weaving and pottery-making.

The culture of our forebears underwent a corresponding shift. Neolithic people had a wealth of zoological and botanical knowledge, and were experts at some forms of agriculture and pastoralism. Their imagination did not stop at the limits of their everyday world; their worldview was embracing in its dimensions and animistic and spiritualistic in its substance. Spirit was not separated from matter, nor was the real world from the dream world. The forces of nature were also the forces of the spirits embodied in objects, plants, animals, and people. The entire world had a sacred dimension. Forces outside and above humans acted in and on the world, having an impact on nature as well as on human communities. People viewed themselves as belonging to a dynamic universe, with seen and unseen forces and entities. Consequently, Paleolithic communities could achieve a high level of integration. The individual was an essential part of the clan or tribe, which in turn was embedded in nature and governed by cosmic forces. Nature and humans did not exist in separation, much less in opposition.

The varieties of "lithic" belief systems were suited to people's ways of life and their relations to nature. At the Paleolithic food-gathering and hunting-fishing stage, the male principle dominated, consistent with the survival priorities and needs of the times. Subsequently, at the agricultural-based Neolithic stage of food production, the female principle became dominant, reflecting the new relations of the herder and farmer to the soil and the Earth. Earth-oriented fecundity and fertility, sexual symbolism, and magical-religious rites were remarkably similar among widely separated peoples. They found analogous expression in the Old World in Asia and the Middle East and in the New World of Mesoamerica.

The seemingly infinite endurance of stone-age societies came to an end when the gradual improvement of their tool-based technologies changed people's relations to nature. Neolithic people congregated primarily in major river valleys, where their use of large amounts of water in improved irrigation systems generated massive increments of crops. Metals such as copper and bronze came into use, new methods for measuring the boundaries of lands were discovered, and calendars for reckoning time and writing for recording and communicating messages were invented. This led to population growth and greater complexity of social organization and placed a greater load on the environment.

In some regions of the Fertile Crescent, such as Sumer, trees were chopped down, soil was overworked, and the climate became arid. But Neolithic communities fanned out, working vaster lands and drawing on the resources of a larger environment. Many villages grew into towns. In time, some became empires with extended administrative and power structures. A new elite came to inhabit the urban centers. The tribal circle of stone-age communities yielded to the stratified pyramid of the formally organized state characterized by a hierarchical structure and strict discipline. Such were the empires that appeared in Babylonia and in Egypt, China, and India.

The new structures and orders mirrored, and in turn reinforced, the transformation of people's values and worldviews. As fresh emphasis was placed on male dominance, in line with higher socioeconomic stratification, the Earth Mother was subordinated to "sky gods." Territorial rights came to dominate over traditional kinship ties, reflecting increased concern with individual and communal property and a more complex division of labor.

The emerging worldview accounted for the origins and justified the orders of these archaic civilizations. The world was thought to have come into existence as order out of chaos. This was followed by a further distillation of order in the heavens, mirrored by emerging orders on Earth. The cosmos was an organic polity in its own right, possessing both sovereignty and power, and maintaining order and harmony throughout the reaches of the universe. Its powers had been created and were wielded by a supreme being, or else by a hierarchy of deities.

People looked to the heavens rather than to the earth for guidance. They were ruled by kings who claimed divine descent and were related to the celestial spheres populated by a pantheon of deities. The celestial orders above called for a theocratic order below. On the principle "as above, so below," human life expanded into a network of relations that extended from the deepest layers of living and nonliving nature to the highest spheres of the heavens.

In theocratic societies, kings ruling by divine fiat embodied and legitimized the exercise of celestially authorized power. Cosmic godship and earthly kingship were united in the intent to maintain an embracing order where the order below reflected the order people believed to reign above. In these societies, the supreme aim was the maintenance of the essential balance of the universe through a social order rooted in cosmic principles. These elements, with but local variations, appeared in ancient Egypt, Mesopotamia, India, and China, as well as in Mesoamerica. They consolidated the centuries-long transformation from the Stone Age of Mythos to a world oriented toward the search for divine order: the world of Theos.

Transformation from Theos to Logos

Even though it was bolstered and underpinned by an elaborate and entrenched culture complete with an enshrined worldview, values, and ethics, the civilization of Theos yielded in time to another civilization, dominated by different beliefs and guided by different values.

This transformation originated with the introduction of iron technology in the theocratic civilizations. In the second millennium B.C.E., Indo-European peoples equipped with iron technology swept out of Central Asia in several directions. Some came through the Khyber Pass into India, where they put an end to the already enfeebled Indus civilization. Others moved southwest into what was then Persia, and still others penetrated to the Black Sea and Eastern Europe, migrating north along the Volga or west along the Danube and the Rhine. Still others settled on the northern coast of the Mediterranean, on the Greek and Italian peninsulas. In time, the settlements gave rise to the Greek city-states and to the Greco-Roman civilization. The former extended, under Alexander, to the limits of the then known world, and the latter, under the emperors, stretched from Britain to the Tigris-Euphrates and the Sahara.

The technologies of these civilizations triggered change in their social structure, and these changes were reflected in corresponding shifts in values and beliefs. In classical Hellas, the great nature philosophers developed a new view of the world. They replaced mythical concepts with theories based on observation and elaborated by reasoning. The pre-Socratic thinkers evolved the "heroic mind," present in Homer and the early epics, into the visionary and the theoretical mind, in a process that culminated with Socrates in the rational mind that was then epitomized by Plato and Aristotle. Logos—a term that originally meant "word" but came to mean rational discourse and even rationality itself—became the central concept, at the heart of philosophy as well as of religion. Together with the concept of quantitative measure, *metron,* it provided Western civilization with the intellectual foundation on which it was to build for nearly two and a half millennia.

Logos, as embodied by classical Greco-Roman civilization, was not a purely quantitative worldview, devoid of qualitative elements. Humans, and to some extent all creatures, had special worth or virtue, *arete,* not accountable for in terms of quantitative properties alone. The combination of logos and metron with arete constituted a worldview, an ethic, and a system of values that was altogether different from the Theos-civilization of the archaic empires. Man was the measure, and the unfolding of human potentials was the goal. This basic notion, with many sophisticated variants, came to flower in the philosophical systems of the Hellenic thinkers and found application in the organization of Greek city-states. Many of its elements carried over into Roman civilization, which was endowed with a pragmatic orientation keyed to the powerful maintenance of order through the orderly exercise of power.

After the fall of the Western Empire and the founding of the Eastern (Byzantine) Empire in the year 476 C.E., a further shift occurred in the ways of life, culture, and organization of European societies. The rise of Christianity modified the classical culture of Logos. Christianity added to the traditional concepts a divine source believed to be the world's creator, prime mover, as well as ultimate judge. Logos came to be embodied in the Holy Trinity and incarnated in man, God's creation. Medieval Logos, the principal elements of which Augustine and Thomas Aquinas elaborated, was the hallmark of European civilization until the advent of the modern age.

A further shift occurred in the mindset of Europe in the sixteenth and seventeenth centuries. It built on the rationality of the Greeks, borrowed and elaborated by the Romans. This rationality was conserved in medieval fiefdoms and princedoms notwithstanding the addition of Christian elements. It found expression outside medieval monasteries in the creation and use of mechanical devices such as clocks, windmills, water mills, animal-drawn agricultural implements, and horse-drawn carriages.

In the seventeenth century, Europe's mechanically colored Logos culminated in Galileo's concept of the world as a giant machine. Newton's mathematical demonstration of the universality of the laws of motion confirmed Galileo's concept and provided a basis for an embracing worldview that became the decisive feature of the modern world. The new concept took hold on the Continent as well as on the British Isles. It accounted for the behavior of bodies on Earth by mechanical principles, the same as for the movement of the heavens. The universe was a divinely designed clockwork that was set in motion by a prime mover and then ran harmoniously through all eternity. It was believed to operate according to strict laws of nature. A knowledge of these laws was said to enable the rational mind to know all things past, present, and future. The place of God in this system was restricted to being its "prime mover." As the French mathematician Pierre-Simone Laplace is reputed to have replied to Napoleon, God was a hypothesis for which there was no longer any need.

At first, there was open conflict between the medieval theistic Logos imposed by the Church and the mechanistic and naturalistic Logos that emerged in lay society. But inquiry into the nature of the world independent of religious dogma soon took off. Church and science learned to coexist; an accommodation was reached. The Church claimed for itself the domain of "moral philosophy" (which embraced what later came to be called the social sciences and the humanities) and science had the field of "natural philosophy" (which corresponded to the contemporary concept of natural science). This accommodation was a socially useful development, because the conception of the natural world as a giant and reliable mechanism was a counterweight to the disunity of the warring princedoms. It offered a more secure orientation for human aspirations than what Galileo called "the passions that divide the minds of men."

In nineteenth-century Europe and America, the scientific worldview became the dominant feature of civilization. Darwin's theory of evolution completed the mechanistic concept of Newtonian physics; it accounted for the evolution of life from simple origins through the mechanism of random mutations exposed to the test of natural selection. The worldview that emerged was "purified" and "objective," believed to be free of subjective and emotional preconceptions. In the influential heritage of French philosopher René Descartes, human consciousness is the sole indubitable reality (*cogito ergo sum*—I think therefore I am). Only consciousness is indubitable: It is the *res cogitans* (the thinking substance). The natural world is only inferred: It is *res extensa* (extended substance). It then follows that we humans, the sole entities endowed with mind and consciousness, are free to exploit the machinelike, merely extended world around us for purposes of our own. In the words of Francis Bacon, we are free to wrest nature's secrets from her bosom for our benefit.

This mechanistic-materialistic Logos spread in the eighteenth and nineteenth centuries from Europe to America, and in the twentieth century from America to the rest of the world.

What can we learn from these civilizational transformations? We see that each kind of civilization had its own kind of culture and consciousness. The age of Mythos was hallmarked by mythical consciousness; the age of Theos by a theistic mindset; and the European Middle Ages by a theistically colored Logos. The modern age, in turn, evolved a mechanistic and manipulative Logos. These cultures and mindsets were useful and functional in their time. Indeed, the reason civilization could evolve rather than go under is because better forms of thinking arose from time to time. Of course, they did not arise everywhere and in all times: Countless civilizations did fail to survive, victims of changing conditions to which they could not adapt. But the civilizations that did survive had a new mindset.

Einstein was right: the problems created by the prevalent way of thinking cannot be solved by the same way of thinking. This is a crucial insight. Without renewing our culture and consciousness we will be unable to transform today's dominant civilization and overcome the problems generated by its shortsighted mechanistic and manipulative thinking.

The Challenge of the Next Transformation

The road on which we find ourselves is about to divide. In the span of the next few years the evolution of our civilization will take a new direction. Can we make sure that it takes a good direction?

Finding a positive direction for the next transformation of civilization is a challenging but not an insuperable task. We know that a viable new civilization must evolve a culture and consciousness very different from the mindset that characterized most of the twentieth century. Logos-inspired civilization was materialistic and manipulative, driven by the search for wealth and power. The alternative to it is civilization centered on human development, and the development of the communities and the environments in which humans live their lives.

Two Kinds of Growth

The change in direction we need can be grasped in reference to the kind of growth to which a civilization and its people are dedicated. Growth is not necessarily bad or even limited: The desirability and the future of growth depend on what *kind* of growth we are embarking upon. Unrestrained, purely quantitative growth in energy and materials production and consumption is not possible on a finite planet with a delicately balanced biosphere—ultimately it is bound to turn into growth of a cancerous kind. But there are other forms of growth we could aim for. We can distinguish two principal kinds: one is "extensive growth" and the other "intensive growth."

Extensive growth moves along a horizontal plane on the surface of the planet: It conquers ever more territories, colonizes ever more people, and imposes the will of the dominant layers on ever more layers of the population. Intensive growth, on the other hand, centers on the development of individuals, and of the communities and ecologies in which they live. Extensive growth generates unsustainability: It drives the world toward chaos. Intensive growth could produce sustainability: It could drive contemporary societies toward a new mode of functioning—a new civilization.

The ends and the means of extensive and intensive growth are radically different. The basic end of extensive growth is the extension of human power over larger and larger areas. Traditionally, the means to achieve this end has been conquest: the conquest of nature and the conquest of other, weaker or less power- and domination-oriented peoples. Successful conquest led to the colonization of other tribes, nations, cities, and empires, subjugating them to the ambitions and interests of the conquerors. For most of recorded history, this was accomplished by force of arms. Since the second half of the twentieth century, it has been also attempted by economic means, using the power of wealthy states and global business companies to impose their will and values on wide layers of the population.

For states, the goal of extensive growth is territorial sovereignty, including sovereignty over the human and natural resources of the territories. The corresponding goal for global companies is to generate demand for consumption, often without much regard for the social and environmental consequences.

The paramount end of extensive growth can be encapsulated in three "C's": *conquest, colonization,* and *consumption.* This end is served by corresponding varieties of means: first, the technologies that use and transform matter, the technologies of *production;* second, the technologies that generate the power to operate matter-transforming technologies, *energy-generating* technologies; and third, the technologies that whet people's appetite, create artificial demand, and shift patterns of consumption, the technologies of *propaganda, public relations, and advertising.* The first of these kinds of technologies built habitations with networks of transportation and communication and increasingly powerful production structures for a growing variety of products. The second harnessed the forces of nature to drive these technologies. And the third produced the demand-provoking images and the subtle or not-so-subtle means by which the producers of products and services impose their will on clients and customers.

In intensive growth, the end is very different. It can be grasped under three other "C's": *connection, communication,* and *consciousness.*

Let us take connection first. One of the great myths of the Industrial Age has been the skin-enclosed separation of individuals from each other and the disjunction of their interests from the interests of others. The former aspect of this myth has been legitimized by the worldview based on classical physics. Like the mass points of Newton, humans appeared to be self-contained, mutually independent chunks of organized matter only externally related to each other and to their environment. Classical economics reinforced this myth by viewing the individual as a self-centered economic actor, pursuing his or her own interests on the comforting assumption that it harmonized with the interests of others thanks to the workings of the market. But, as we shall see in chapter 6, the contemporary sciences no longer support such views. Now every quantum is known to be subtly connected with every other quantum, and every organism with other organisms in the ecosystem. In turn, economists know that there is a direct connection between the interests of individuals, individual states, and individual enterprises and the workings of the globalized international system. In our world, these embracing connections evolve rapidly, and it is one of the ends of intensive growth to order them, creating coherent structure in place of random proliferation.

The second aim of intensive growth, directly linked with the first, deepens the level of communication and raises the level of consciousness of the communicators.

Communication unfolds on multiple levels. First of all, we need to communicate with ourselves, caring for and developing our consciousness and personality. People who are "in touch with themselves" are more balanced and more able to communicate with the world around them. We also need to be in communication with those who make up the immediate context of our lives—family, community, and coworkers or professional colleagues. Still wider levels of communication are equally necessary: communication with other people, whether near or far, in our own community and in other communities, countries, and cultures.

Communication calls for connection, but on the human plane more enters into play than connection: communication also involves *consciousness*. The full potential of human communication unfolds when the communicators apprehend the strands of connection through which they communicate. A high level of communication requires a high level of consciousness that enables people to make use of the many, sometimes extremely subtle, strands of connection that bind them to each other and to their environment. Consciousness of these connections lifts human thinking from the outdated ego-centered level to the urgently needed community-, ecology-, and planet-centered dimension.

Evolution focused on the growth of connection, communication, and consciousness could create a fundamental shift in the civilization that dominates life on this planet. It could drive the next transformation in a positive direction: from Logos to *Holos*.

5

The Image of a New Civilization

If we shift from the extensive to the intensive form of growth, the Chaos Point we will reach at the end of 2012 and in the years beyond will not lead to breakdown. The outdated and increasingly counterproductive mechanistic-manipulative Logos of industrial civilization will be replaced by a more adapted mindset. In the optimum case, this will lead to a civilization that merits the name *Holos* ("wholeness" in classical Greek). Holos civilization will be a planetary civilization hallmarked by the kind of thinking that enables people to see not just the trees in front of them, but the forest that is now their planetary habitat.

What would a holistic civilization look like—how would it be to live in it? Here is an image of the worldviews, the life ways, the morality, the decision-making and security structures, and, last but not least, the consciousness that would characterize the holistic civilization we could create on this planet by the year 2032.

Dateline: 2032

Worldviews 2032

In this third decade of the twenty-first century, the view people hold of themselves, of nature, and of the cosmos is still culturally colored and hence diverse, but it is united in rejecting the mechanistic and fragmented concept of world and self that was the heritage of the Industrial Age. A new view is emerging:

Humans are organic wholes within an organic biosphere in the embrace of an organically evolving universe. The emerging view is supported by the experience of people who seek wholeness in their personal development, the same as in their social and community relations and in relations with nature.

The new worldview is a sharp contrast to the worldview that dominated the Industrial Age. People no longer believe they are free to manipulate the environment as they wish, in the hope that the consequences will take care of themselves or new technologies will take care of them. They also do not believe that life is a struggle for survival, where fitness is rightfully rewarded by wealth and power. And the classical mechanistic view of reality is likewise transcended: The universe, people realize, is not a passive backdrop to human actions, and individual actions have an immediate, even if not always immediately evident, impact on the environment. Subtle ties, people know, bind human beings to one another, to the biosphere, and to the cosmos as a whole. They know that what we do to others and to nature, we also do to ourselves.

Life Ways 2032

People live more simply than those who could afford a luxurious lifestyle lived in the late twentieth and early twenty-first century. Simpler lifestyles are not imposed by poverty, and they are not the consequence of rules and legislations or high taxes, although such measures functioned at first as incentives and continue to function as safeguards. They are the voluntary result of a different mindset. People realize that a high material standard of living does not necessarily mean a high quality of life. Garages filled with luxury cars, closets full of seldom-worn clothes, and stacks of unplayed CDs are not preconditions of happiness. Quite the contrary: A luxurious lifestyle often proved to be stressful and unhealthy. It involved "keeping up with the Joneses" in a race that was independent of how much one has already achieved: People wanted still more.

And when it came to reaping the benefits of affluence, a life of luxury was seldom a path to the good life. Lounging in the sun, smoking a cigarette, sipping a daiquiri, munching on a hamburger, and talking on the cellular phone were wasteful as well as dangerous: These practices increased the chances of getting skin cancer, lung cancer, cirrhosis of the liver, high cholesterol, and brain damage. They were not an improvement over working at a high-pressure job, taking smoke breaks every hour, drinking a martini after work to relax, and going to sleep in front of the television.

People now realize that there are more satisfying ways to spend one's leisure hours. Helping friends and neighbors, doing volunteer work in one's community, enjoying nature, visiting sites of natural, historical, or cultural interest, hiking, swimming, biking, reading, listening to music, or taking an interest in literature and theater are satisfying pursuits that do not involve a high level of material and energy consumption and do not require much money. Yet they are healthier for humans and better for the environment than the Industrial-Age paragon of success, affluence, and luxury.

Individuals in 2032 are healthier and they live longer, but do not trigger a further growth of the population. They realize that it is irresponsible to produce families beyond the replacement level: two children is the indicated family size in most parts of the globe. Population growth is stabilizing at a sustainable level. This brings notable benefits: With modest family size, parents are able to care better for their children, ensuring that they grow into healthy individuals with sufficient resources and education to live well and responsibly.

Life ways are becoming ecologically sustainable. People are reoriented from aiming at external growth to focusing on internal growth, shifting from aiming at conquest and consumption to wishing to further the evolution of their thinking and behavior and the development of their communities. Thus energy and material requirements have become more modest and energy and materials use more efficient. People work together to improve their shared living and working space—community life enjoys a renaissance. There is a renaissance of spirituality as well; women and men are rediscovering a higher or deeper dimension of their lives and existence.

Morality 2032

Diversity is joined with unity also in the area of morality. As ethical concerns move from the margin of holiday sermons and weekend discussions to the center of everyday life, moral considerations inform the decisions people make in the private sphere as well as in the sphere of business and profession.

The ethics of a person's behavior is still assessed in light of the values and beliefs of his or her community and culture, but beyond the diversity of moral conceptions there is a deeper unity: People agree that it is immoral to live in ways that reduce access for others to the resources required for a life of basic dignity and well-being. The new morality is rooted in a universal principle: Live and act in a way that enables others to live as well. Live not necessarily in the same way, but with a real possibility of satisfying basic needs and pursuing the ends of well-being and happiness.

Following the example of nature as a self-evolving integral system rather than an arena for life-or-death struggle, the new ethics replaces cutthroat competition with spirited rivalry in the context of shared values and interests. This makes for more conscious and responsible consumer behavior, with a preference for products with low-material and high-information content, and for services that guide and facilitate personal development. It brings an improvement in the quality of life without creating an increment in the material requirements of life.

Decision-Making and Security 2032

The political world is globalized, but it is locally diverse; it is networked, but not monolithic. Sovereign nation-states, the inheritance of the modern age, have given way to a transnational system organized as a Chinese box of decision-making forums, with each forum having its own sphere of authority and responsibility.

Decision-making at the different levels is not subordinate to a higher or to the highest level. In some areas—including trade and finance, information and communication, peace and security, and environmental protection—decisions are taken on the global level. But this still allows significant autonomy at local, national, and regional levels. The 2032 world-system is not a hierarchy but a "heterarchy": a multilevel sequentially integrated structure of distributed decision-making. It is aimed at global coordination combined with regional, national, and local self-determination.

The new system is made up of a sequence of autonomous communities, linked by multiple strands of communication and cooperation. Citizens and citizen-groups jointly shape and develop their community. Local communities participate in a wider network of cooperation that includes, but does not cease at, the level of national states. Nation-states are part of regional social and economic federations, coming together in the United Peoples Organization, the world body resulting from the reform of the United Nations. Its members are not nation-states but the continental and subcontinental federations that integrate the relevant aspects and shared interests of nations. The regional bodies include the European Federation, the North American Federation, the Latin American Federation, the North-African Middle-Eastern Federation, the Sub-Saharan African Federation, the Central Asian Federation, the South and Southeast Asian Federation, and the Australian-Asia-Pacific Federation.

In the new system of decision-making, the principle of subsidiarity is observed: Decisions are made on the lowest level at which they are effective.

The *global level* is the highest level of decision-making, yet it is also the lowest level at which peace and security can be ensured and the global flow of goods, money, and technology can be monitored. It is the level for coordinating the information that flows on globe-spanning channels of communication, and the level at which regional and national policies aimed at safeguarding the integrity of the biosphere can be harmonized.

The *regional level* is indicated for decisions that coordinate the social and political aspirations and concerns of nations within the given regions. Regional economic and social organizations provide the forum for the elected representatives of member nations to consider and harmonize the interests and aspirations of their populations.

The *national level* is appropriate for most of the functions traditionally performed by national governments, but without claiming absolute sovereignty for their nation-state and with due regard for decisions made in other forums, above as well as below the level of their state.

The *local level* of decision-making brings together the elected representatives of urban and rural communities. They coordinate the workings of the social and political institutions of towns, villages, and rural regions in direct consultation with their inhabitants.

Responsibility for security is vested in the regional federations. Large and expensive national armies with vast and dangerous arsenals have been abolished. Each federation maintains a small standing army drawn from and financed by its member states. In the absence of national armies, the danger of one state attacking another has diminished, and joint peacekeeping forces can handle any potentially threatening situation.

National governments remain in charge of internal security, which they ensure through police forces and national guards. External security is entrusted to the federations jointly constituted by nations in their region. This frees considerable human and financial resources for socially and humanly beneficial ends. The benefits of such "peace dividends" were known for decades, but they could not be attained until the threat to security had lessened. First, the smaller and more prosperous countries embraced the project of joint peacekeeping, then the poorer countries, and finally also the former nuclear powers: Russia, China, England, France, and the United States.

Consciousness 2032

There are many things that differentiate people in the year 2032: religious beliefs, cultural heritage, economic and technological development, climate, and environment. But a new consciousness enables them to agree on principles that truly matter:

- That it is immoral for anyone to live in a way that detracts from the chances of others to achieve a life of basic well-being and human dignity
- That it is better to exercise responsible trusteeship of the human and natural sources of wealth on this planet than to exploit them for narrow and short-term benefit
- That nature is not a mechanism to be engineered and exploited, but a living system that brought us into being, that nourishes us, and, given our awesome powers of exploitation and destruction, is now entrusted to our care
- That the way to solve problems and conflicts is not by attacking each other, but by understanding one another and cooperating in ways that serve the shared interest
- That the universal rights adopted by foresighted people in the twentieth century—the right to freedom of expression, freedom to elect our leaders, and freedom from torture and other arbitrary constraints on personal liberty, as well as the right to food, shelter, education, and employment—apply to everyone in the world, and deserve to be respected above and beyond considerations of personal, ethnic, and national self-interest.

PART TWO

BUILDING THE NEW CIVILIZATION

6

The Emerging Foundations

We live at a time when we have the unprecedented power—and hence the unprecedented responsibility—to decide our destiny. We face the specter of a global breakdown—economic, social, as well as ecological—but it is not fated: We have the option of taking a brighter path. We have a window in time, a few years to avert breakdown and build a civilization capable of bringing peace, sustainability, and an acceptable level of well-being to all people on this planet.

Nothing is keeping us from shifting our evolutionary path toward a peaceful and sustainable civilization but our will and vision. Mainstream society has not yet mustered these essential human resources, but that does not mean that they are lacking. The kind of foundation we need to create a holistic new civilization is already emerging at the creative frontiers of society.

Holism in the New Cultures

The word "culture" means here the ensemble of the values, worldviews, aspirations, and customs that characterize a people and distinguish it from others. This is what we mean when we speak of Western culture, indigenous cultures, Eastern cultures, and also of a holistic culture, or a culture of nonviolence. When we define culture in this way, it is evident that a variety of new cultures are on the rise. They are "subcultures" (or "alternative cultures") for they differ from the culture of the mainstream. This is not exceptional: Societies are seldom culturally monolithic. In times of innovation and ferment, a large number of alternative cultures may coexist with the culture of the establishment.

One of the alternative cultures in industrial societies is particularly interesting. It is made up of people who are rethinking their preferences, priorities, values, and behaviors, shifting from consumption based on quantity toward selectivity in view of quality defined by environmental friendliness, sustainability, and the ethics of production and use. In this culture, lifestyles of matter- and energy-wasteful ostentation are shifting toward modes of living hallmarked by voluntary simplicity and the search for a new morality and harmony with nature.

These changes in values and behaviors, though generally disregarded or underestimated by decision-takers, are rapid and revolutionary. They are occurring in all segments of society, but most intensely at the margins. Here a number of grassroots movements are opting out of the mainstream and are reforming themselves. These groups are barely visible, since for the most part their members go about their business without trying to convert others or call attention to themselves. They underestimate their own numbers and lack social organization and political cohesion. Yet the more serious and sincere of these cultures merit recognition. Unlike esoteric cultures and sects, members of these cultures do not engage in antisocial activities, indulge in promiscuous sex, or seek isolation. Rather, they rethink accepted beliefs, values, and life ways and strike out on new paths of personal and social behavior to the best of their insight and possibility.

The people who join these groups are united by the aspiration to live a more simple, healthy, whole, and ethical life. They are appalled by what they see as the heartless impersonality and mindless destructiveness of establishment society. The rise of inner-city deprivation and violence, the drift toward anarchy and ethnic intolerance, the impotence of police and military measures to cope with it, the dissolution of the social contract between society and worker, and the rise of unemployment and homelessness prompt them to change their thinking and priorities.

California's Institute of Noetic Sciences found that the changes that occur in America's hopeful subculture include these shifts in values and behavior:

- The shift from competition to reconciliation and partnership
- The shift from greed and scarcity to sufficiency and caring

- The shift from outer to inner authority—from reliance on outer sources of "authority" to inner sources of "knowing"
- The shift from mechanistic to living systems—from concepts of the world modeled on mechanistic systems, to perspectives and approaches rooted in the principles that inform the realms of life
- And, perhaps most significant of all, the shift from separation to wholeness—a fresh recognition of the wholeness and interconnectedness of all aspects of life and reality

An important shift occurs in the area of consumer behavior. In *Megatrends 2010* (a book that, despite its title, deals not with the extrapolation of dominant trends but with the rise of a radically new movement that promises to evolve into a major trend), Patricia Aburdene traces the rise of what she calls "conscious capitalism." It appears in the market in the form of conscious, or value-driven, consumption. By the turn of the century, the market in the United States for value-driven commerce had reached $230 billion; the New York Times called it "the biggest market you have never heard of." Conscious consumers, often referred to as LOHAS (Lifestyles of Health and Sustainability) consumers, make up a rapidly growing segment in five sectors of the economy:

- The sustainability sector, including ecologically sound construction, renewable energy technologies, and socially responsible investments
- The healthy living sector, appearing in the market as demand for natural and organic foods, nutritional supplements, and personal care
- The alternative healthcare sector, comprised of wellness centers and complementary and alternative medical services and health care
- The personal development sector, made up of seminars, courses, and shared experiences in the body-mind-spirit area;
- The ecological life-culture sector, appearing in the form of demand for ecologically produced, recycled or recyclable products, as well as ecotourism

Such shifts in the culture and behavior of a growing number of people merit serious consideration. Yet mainstream society seldom differentiates between the more and the less sincere and serious elements of the alternative cultures, viewing them with mistrust. The labels "esoteric" and "New Age" are frequently applied to people who espouse alternative values and lifestyles; the establishment brands them as marginal or, if it takes serious notice, considers them a threat to law and order. This is unfortunate. Dismissing and distrusting people who do not accept the prevalent system of values and the associated worldviews and lifestyles is naive and indiscriminate. It is true that some alternative cultures are escapist, introverted, and narcissistic, but the more genuine among them have a core of values and priorities that is highly promising for a positive result of the coming Chaos Point. To dismiss these cultures is to throw out the baby with the bathwater.

In the United States, at the center of the industrialized world, a holistically oriented alternative culture is growing rapidly. This is the surprising conclusion of a series of opinion surveys carried out recently by organizations and individuals intent on tracing the evolution of the thinking and acting of Americans.

The California-based Fund for Global Awakening implemented a survey aimed at elucidating the common values and beliefs held by people of diverse backgrounds. Carried out in the framework of the "In Our Own Words 2000 Research Program," the survey distinguished eight "American types." It found that of the 1,600 respondents—selected so as to represent a cross-section of American society—14.4 percent are centered in a material world, 14.2 percent are disengaged from social concerns, 12.1 percent embrace traditional values, and 10 percent are cautious and conservative. These make up half of the U.S. population: the conservative, traditional half. Another 11.9 percent seek to connect to others through self-exploration, 9.4 percent persist through adversity, 11.6 percent seek community transformation, and 16.4 percent work for what the survey defines as a "new life of wholeness." These make up the more creative and (at least in part) change-oriented half. Those who seek community transformation and work for a new life of wholeness make up 28 percent of the people.

The findings of the Fund for Global Awakening match the results of another survey of lifestyles and consumption patterns in the U.S., the American Lives Survey, carried out periodically since the early 1990s. Principal researcher Paul Ray calls the members of America's particularly hopeful alternative culture "cultural creatives." The culture of the creatives contrasts with the culture of the "traditionals." The traditionals are people who wish to opt out of the mainstream by harking back to bygone times.

The mainstream of the U.S. population is made up of what Ray terms the "moderns." The moderns are stalwart supporters of consumer society; their culture is that of the office towers and factories of big business and of the banks and stock markets. Their values are those taught in America's most prestigious schools and colleges. At the turn of the twenty-first century, this was the culture of some 48 percent of the American people: 93 million out of about 193 million adults, more men than women. The family income of this sector was $40,000 to $50,000 per year, situating moderns in the middle- to upper-income bracket.

The Moderns

The *moderns* have many of the positive virtues and values typical of Americans: honesty, the importance of family and education, belief in God and a fair day's pay for a fair day's work. But they also have values and beliefs that distinguish them from the alternative U.S. cultures. These include:

• Making or having a lot of money
• Climbing the ladder of success with measurable steps toward one's goals
• "Looking good" or being stylish
• Being on top of the latest trends and innovations
• Being entertained by the media

For the most part, moderns believe that:

• The body is much like a machine.
• Organizations, too, are very much like machines.
• Either big business or big government is in control and knows best.
• Bigger is better.
• What can be measured is what gets done.
• Analyzing things—dissecting parts—is the best way to solve a problem.
• Efficiency and speed are top priorities (time is money).
• Life can be compartmentalized into separate spheres: work, family, social-izing, making love, education, politics, and religion.
• Being concerned with spirituality and the inner dimensions of life is "flaky" and immaterial to the real business of living.

The Traditionals

In 1999, the *traditionals* made up 24.5 percent of the U.S. population: 48 million adults. They came from a variety of socioeconomic and ethnic backgrounds, with family incomes in the relatively low range of $20,000 to \$30,000 per year, due among other things to the diminished income of the many retirees among them. Demographically, they are older and less educated than the other two U.S. population segments. More than two-thirds are religious conservatives who oppose abortion. The politics of the Bush1 and Bush2 regimes have swollen their ranks by encouraging the growth of the controversial mindset known as Christian fundamentalism.

The thinking of the traditionals is very different from the thinking of the moderns. Traditionals are outraged about the disappearance of the small-town way of life they claim to remember and now hark back to. Some among them take the small-town Main Street business stance against big-business Wall Street ethics; others harbor the traditional working-class resentment of big and wealthy corporations. Their culture has an element of nostalgia for the values and lifestyles they believe characterized America in the past.

- Patriarchs should dominate family life.
- "Feminism" is a swearword: Men need to keep to their traditional roles, and women to theirs.
- Men should be proud to serve their country in the military.
- Freedom to carry arms is essential for everyone.
- Family, church, and community are where everybody belongs.
- The conservative version of whichever religion one belongs to is the correct one.
- All the guidance one needs in life can be found in the Bible.
- Customary and familiar ways of life should be maintained.
- Rural and small-town life is more virtuous than big-city and suburban life.
- Sex should be regulated; this includes pornography, teen sex, and extramarital sex.
- Abortion is a sin against life.
- The country should do more to support virtuous behavior.
- Restricting and punishing immoral behavior is more important than ensuring civil liberties.
- Foreigners and foreign things are an unwelcome presence.

The Cultural Creatives

The *cultural creatives,* the truly hopeful U.S. alternative culture, consists of people from the middle to the wealthy classes, more women than men.

According to Ray, at the turn of the century, the share of this culture was 23.4 percent of the U.S. adult population—slightly less than the 28 percent found subsequently by the In Our Own Words (IOOW) survey.

The cultural creatives are united less by what they preach than by what they practice, for they seldom attempt to convert others, preferring to be concerned with their own personal growth. Their behavior, especially their lifestyle choices, differentiates them from the other cultures.

Books and radio: Cultural creatives (CCs) buy more books and magazines and listen to more radio, preferably news and classical music, and watch less television than any other group.

Arts and culture: Many CCs are determined consumers of the arts and culture; they are likely to go out and get involved, whether as amateurs or as professionals.

Authenticity: CCs want real, "authentic" goods and services. They have led the consumer rebellion against products considered fake, imitation, throwaway, cliché, or merely fashionable.

Selective consumption: CCs do not buy on impulse but research what they consume, reading labels and assuring themselves that they are getting what they want. Many are typical consumers of the "experience industry," which offers intense, enlightening, or enlivening experience rather than a specific material product (weekend workshops, spiritual gatherings, personal growth experiences, experiential vacations, and so on). With regard to nonexperiential products, they prefer ecologically sound, efficient goods to mere style and comfort (for instance, ecologically sound high-mileage recyclable cars with top customer service).

Soft innovation: CCs do not simply buy the latest gadgets and innovations on the market; many creatives are slow to get on the Internet. They tend to be innovators and opinion leaders for knowledge-intensive products such as magazines, and fine wines and foods.

Eating habits: The creatives are "foodies"; they like to talk about food, experiment with new kinds of food, eat out or cook with friends, trying gourmet, ethnic, and natural health foods.

Home styles: CCs buy fewer new houses than people of their income level in other groups because they view the available housing unsuited to their lifestyle. Instead, they mostly buy resale houses and fix them up to their liking. They avoid status displays with impressive columns and entrances, preferring inward-looking spaces hidden by fences and shrubbery. They want their home to be a "nest," with many interesting nooks and niches. CCs like to work at home and often convert a bedroom or den into a home office.

"Whole process" information: CCs want the "whole process" story of whatever they get in their hands, from cereal boxes to product descriptions to magazine articles. They dislike superficial advertising and product description, wanting to know how things originated, how they were made, who made them, and what will happen to them when they are discarded.

Social activism: The creatives view themselves as synthesizers and healers, not just on the personal level but also on the community and the national levels, even on the planetary level. They aspire to create change in personal values and public behaviors that could shift the dominant culture beyond the materialistic and fragmented world of the moderns.

Holism: The most fundamental feature of the culture of the creatives is their holism. This comes to the fore in their preference for natural whole foods, holistic health care, holistic inner experience, whole-system information, and holistic balance between work and play, consumption and inner growth.

The moderns constitute the most populous and change-resistant segment of the U.S. population. The segment of the traditionals is shrinking: As older members die, they are not being replaced by nearly as many younger people as they were previously. In contrast, the population of cultural creatives is growing. Twenty years ago, the CCs made up less than 3 percent of the total American population, but at the turn of the century they totaled about 50 million people—and their numbers appear to be growing.

The growth of the CC subculture is at the same time the growth of the holistic mindset in America, and presumably in other countries as well. A survey carried out in late 2005 by the Italian branch of the Club of Budapest found that about 35 percent of Italians live and act as cultural creatives. Similar figures have come to light in the surveys of the Club of Budapest in Italy, Hungary, and Japan.

In an article in the May–June 2005 issue of *Resurgence*, William Bloom, head of the UK-based Holistic Network, noted, "The holistic approach is rapidly becoming a major cultural force. There is substantial and rigorously researched evidence that the majority of the population in the United Kingdom, and other industrialized and democratized nations, is adopting a holistic worldview." In a modern way, he said, holism catches the most profound spiritual instincts: to become a fulfilled and whole human being; to create healthy and whole communities, local and global; to include and care for all elements and dimensions; to connect with and feel that we are part of the whole meaning and mystery of existence.

The rise of a holistic subculture is a vital sign of hope in our critical times. It indicates the emergence of a solid foundation for a sustainable new civilization—a civilization where people think and behave as responsible citizens of our home planet.

Holism in the New Sciences

Science's emerging view of man, nature, and universe is distinctly holistic. It converges with the intuitive holism of the alternative cultures and completes and complements the emerging foundations of a new civilization.

Science's emerging holism captures the pathbreaking ideas of South African statesman and philosopher Jan Smuts. In his 1926 book *Holism and Evolution,* Smuts wrote that holism is "the principle which works up the raw material or unorganized energy units of the world, utilizes and organizes them, endows them with specific structure and character and individuality, and finally with personality, and creates beauty and truth and value for them." In this sense, holism, said Smuts, is "the basis of a new *Weltanschauung* [worldview] within the general framework of science."

In Smuts's time, science was materialistic and atomistic: Its principal research method was to take apart the systems it investigated and examine the parts in isolation. Scientists then endeavored to reconstruct the whole system on the basis of the interrelations of its parts. In the case of complex systems—and even an atom with more than one electron orbiting its nucleus is a dynamically complex system—this encountered intractable difficulties. More than 50 years had to pass before the limitations of this endeavor in regard to most of the systems of scientific interest, from atoms to organisms and galaxies, made an impression on the science establishment.

Holism today is present not only as a philosophy "within the general framework of science," to use Smuts's phrase, but as a new fundamental paradigm: a basic hallmark of scientific theories themselves. This brings the new sciences significantly closer to the hopeful subcultures in society, a convergence that is all the more significant as it blazes a trail toward a civilization in which holistic thinking embraces all things in nature and society.

The convergence of science and the emerging cultures marks a new epoch in history. The mechanistic and materialistic mindset of the modern age created a deep gulf between science and intuitive modes of envisioning the world. It obliged people to believe *either* in science *or* in the intuited or revealed wisdom of mysticism and religion. This gulf arose in the Western world at the dawn of the modern age. As already noted, science had legitimacy in the eyes of the late medieval Church if it limited itself to "natural philosophy," leaving "moral philosophy"—all things to do with values, ethics, mind, and soul—to Christian theology. Giordano Bruno was burned at the stake for transgressing this divide, while Galileo managed to escape by making a careful distinction between "primary qualities" such as the solidity of bodies, their extension, figure, number, and motion, and secondary qualities such as color, taste, beauty, or ugliness. He claimed freedom for science only for the investigation of the former.

The separation of the investigation of the material world from reflections on the world of mind and spirit did not prevent great scientists from seeking a relationship between them. The founders of modern science were integral thinkers. Bruno, Galileo, Copernicus, Kepler, and Newton himself had deep intuitive, even mystical streaks. Nor did intuition lack in the giants of twentieth-century science. As their writings testify, it was a leading element in the thinking of Einstein, Erwin Schrödinger, and Niels Bohr, as well as of Wolfgang Pauli and Carl Jung, to mention but a few.

Today the emerging holism of the new sciences offers not only fresh possibilities for overcoming the vexing divide that the English culture historian C. P. Snow called the "two cultures" of Western civilization, but also for lending weight to the kind of thinking that could orient our chaotic world toward a more peaceful and sustainable civilization.

7

What You Can Do Today

A new civilization is not likely to come about in time if we sit with folded hands, waiting for the converging holism of the new cultures and the new sciences to lay the groundwork for it. A critical mass of people in society must take an active role. That means you and me, and others around us.

There are decisive things you and I can do to promote the shift toward a peaceful and sustainable civilization. They include: shedding obsolete beliefs, adopting a new morality, envisioning the world as you would like to see it, and evolving your consciousness.

Shed Obsolete Beliefs

The world today is full of irrational practices. In its Declaration of December 2004, the World Wisdom Council, created at the initiative of the Club of Budapest, queried,

Where is the wisdom in a system that:

- Produces weapons that are more dangerous than the conflicts they are meant to solve?
- Creates an overproduction of food, but fails to make it available to those who are hungry?

- Allows half of the world's children to live in poverty and millions of them to suffer acute hunger?
- Fails to appreciate and make use of the sensitivity, care, and sense of solidarity that women bring to the family and the community, and could bring to politics and business?
- Faces a gamut of tasks and challenges, yet puts more and more people out of work?
- Gives full priority to maximizing the productivity of labor (even though millions are unemployed or underemployed) rather than improving the productivity of resources (notwithstanding that most natural resources are finite and many are scarce and nonrenewable)?
- Requires unrelenting economic and financial growth just to function and not to crash?
- Faces long-term structural and operational problems, yet bases its criteria of success on short-term accounting periods and the day-to-day behavior of stock exchanges?
- Assesses social and economic progress in terms of the gross national product and leaves out of account the quality of life of the people and the level of fulfillment of their basic human needs?
- Fights religious fundamentalism, but enshrines "market fundamentalism" (the belief that unrestrained competition on the market can right all wrongs and solve all problems)?
- Expects people to abide in their private sphere by the golden rule "treat others as you expect to be treated yourself," yet ignores this elementary principle of fairness and equity in politics (to treat other states as you expect other states to treat you) as well as in business (to treat partners and competitors as you expect partners and competitors to treat your company)?

Today's irrational practices are rooted in obsolete beliefs and flawed conceptions, as the short catalog that follows illustrates.

A Catalog of Obsolete Beliefs and Flawed Conceptions

Order through hierarchy: Order in society can only be achieved by rules and laws and their proper enforcement, and this requires a chain of command that is recognized and obeyed by all. A few people on top (mostly males) make up the rules, legislate the laws, give the orders, and ensure compliance with them. Everyone else is to obey the rules and take his or her place within the social and political order.

Everyone is unique and separate: We are all unique and separate individuals enclosed by our skin and pursuing our own interests. As is the case for our business and our country, we have only ourselves to rely on; everyone else is either friend or foe, at best linked to us by ties of mutual (but, alas, mostly short-term) interest.

Everything is reversible: The problems we experience are temporary interludes of perturbation after which everything goes back to normal. All we need to do is manage the difficulties that crop up using tried and tested methods of problem solving and, if necessary, crisis management. Business as unusual has evolved out of business as usual, and sooner or later will reverse back into it.

Why these beliefs are obsolete is not difficult to see.

Male-dominated hierarchies do not work well even in the army and the church, much less in business and society. Successful business managers have learned the advantages of lean structures and teamwork, but for the most part social and political institutions still operate in the traditional hierarchical mode. As a result, governments tend to be heavy-handed, their workings cumbersome and inefficient.

Looking at ourselves as individuals is fine, but considering ourselves separate from the social and the natural world in which we live distorts natural impulses to seek our own advantage into a shortsighted struggle among ever more desperate and unequal competitors. This is a dangerous path to follow, for individuals as well as for states and businesses.

If we remain convinced that the problems we encounter are but temporary disturbances in an unchanging and perhaps unchangeable status quo, no experience of problems will change our thinking and our behavior.

Underlying these obsolete but persistent beliefs are a number of flawed conceptions. They include: economic rationality; the cult of efficiency; technology is the answer; new is better; my country, right or wrong; and the future is none of our business.

Economic rationality: The value of everything, including human beings, can be calculated in monetary terms. Everybody wants to get rich. The rest is idle conversation or simple pretense.

The cult of efficiency: We must get the maximum out of every person, every machine, and every organization regardless of what is produced and whether or not it serves a useful purpose.

63

Technology is the answer: Whatever the problem, technology either can, or can be developed to, offer a solution.

New is better: Anything that is new is better than (almost) anything that is last year's.

My country, right or wrong: Come what may, we owe allegiance only to one flag and one government.

The future is none of our business: Why should we worry about the good of the next generation? Every generation has to look after itself.

Why these conceptions are flawed can be spelled out.

The naive reduction of everything and everybody to economic value may have seemed rational during epochs in which a great economic upswing turned all heads and pushed everything else into the background, but it is foolhardy at a time when people are beginning to rediscover deep-rooted social and spiritual values and to cultivate lifestyles of voluntary simplicity.

Efficiency without regard to what is produced and whom it will benefit leads to mounting unemployment, caters to the demands of the rich without regard to the needs of the poor, and polarizes society into "monetized" and "traditional" sectors.

Technology can be powerful and sophisticated, but it remains a tool: Its utility depends on how it is used. Even the best technology is a two-edged sword. Nuclear reactors produce an almost unlimited supply of energy, but their waste products, as well as decommissioning, pose unsolved problems. Genetic engineering can create virus-resistant and protein-rich plants, improved breeds of animals, vast supplies of animal proteins, and microorganisms capable of producing proteins and hormones and improving photosynthesis; but it can also produce lethal biological weapons and pathogenic microorganisms, destroy the diversity and the balance of nature, and create abnormal, and abnormally aggressive, insects and animals.

Information technologies can create a globally interacting yet locally diverse civilization, enabling all people to be linked whatever their citizenship, culture, and ethnic origin. But when information networks are dominated by the power groups that brought them into being, they serve only the narrow interests of a small minority and marginalize the rest. In the commercialized mode, the Internet, television, and electronic and print media cater to those who can enter the marketplace, and disregard the rest. They also serve criminal elements, propagating pornography and crime.

That the new is always better is simply not true. Often, the new is worse than what it replaced—more expensive, more complex and less manageable, and more wasteful, damaging to health, polluting, alienating, or stressful.

The chauvinistic slogan "my country, right or wrong" ignores the growing cultural, social, and economic ties that evolve among people in different parts of the globe. It asks people to fight for causes their government espouses and may later repudiate, and to embrace the values and worldviews of a small group of political leaders. Nothing in the healthy human mind forbids the expansion of loyalty above the level of a single country; no individual is obliged by his or her emotional makeup to swear exclusive allegiance to one flag only. We can be loyal to several segments of society without being disloyal to any. We can be loyal to our community without giving up loyalty to our province, state, or region. We can be loyal to our region and feel at one with an entire culture and with the human family as a whole. Europeans are English, Germans, French, Spanish, and Italians as well as Europeans. Americans are New Englanders, Texans, Southerners, and Pacific-Northwesterners as well as Americans. People in all parts of the world possess multiple identities and can develop the multiple allegiances that go with them.

Finally, living without conscious forward planning—though it may have been sufficient in days of heady growth, when each new generation could take care of itself—is not a responsible option at a time when the decisions we make today have a profound impact on the well-being of the next generations.

The Particularly Dangerous Beliefs

Nature is inexhaustible. This is the belief that nature around us is an infinite source of resources, and an infinite sink of wastes. Its origins go back to the archaic empires. It would hardly have occurred to the inhabitants of ancient Babylonia, Sumer, Egypt, India, or China that the environment around them could ever be exhausted of the basic necessities of life—edible plants, domestic animals, clean water, and breathable air—or fouled by dumping waste and garbage. The environment must have appeared far too vast to be much affected by what humans did in their small settlements and on the lands that surrounded them. This proved to be a dangerous illusion. In time, it turned much of the Fertile Crescent of biblical times into the Middle East of today: a region with vast areas of arid and infertile land. But in those days, people could move on, colonizing new lands and exploiting fresh resources. Today there is nowhere left to go. In a globally extended industrial civilization wielding powerful technologies, the belief in the inexhaustibility of nature gives free rein to the overuse and thoughtless impairment of the resources of the planet and the unreflective overload of nature's self-regenerative capacities.

The world is a giant mechanism. This dangerous belief dates from the early modern age, a carryover from the Galilean-Newtonian view of the world, according to which simple causes have direct and simple effects. The idea of the world as a giant mechanism was well adapted to creating and operating medieval technologies such as water mills and windmills, pumps, mechanical clocks, and animal-drawn plows and carriages, but it fails when it comes to jet turbines, nuclear reactors, networked computers, and genetically engineered plants and microbes. Sophisticated technologies do not work like Newtonian machines, and they do not have directly calculable effects.

Yet the belief persists that the world around us can be engineered like a machine. The basic notion is that doing one thing can always be relied on to lead predictably to another thing—as pressing a key on an old-fashioned typewriter causes an arm to print the corresponding letter on a sheet of paper. This is no longer the case even for the computer, where sophisticated programs interpret the information entered on the keyboard and decide the result. The mechanistic concept works even worse in interfacing our technologies with nature. The way a transplanted gene is expressed in one plant is foreseeable as regards that plant, but it is problematic when it comes to the interaction of that plant with its environment—and with the humans who consume it. The same gene that produces the foreseen and desired effect in the modified plant can produce unforeseen and undesirable effects in us and in other species.

Nonetheless, twentieth-century industrial civilization persisted in treating both society and nature as a mechanism that can be engineered and reengineered. The result is the progressive degradation of water, air, and soil; the modification of the climate; and the impairment of local and continental ecosystems. The belief that nature is a mechanism, though not as old as the belief that it is inexhaustible, is just as obsolete.

Life is a struggle where only the fittest survive. This belief dates from the nineteenth century, a consequence of the popular understanding of Darwin's theory of natural selection. This concept claims that in society, as in nature, "the fittest survive," meaning that, if we want to survive, we have to be fit for the existential struggle—fitter than others around us. In a societal context, fitness is not determined by genes, but is said to be a personal and cultural trait, such as smartness, daring, ambition, and the political and financial means to put them to work.

Transposing nineteenth-century Darwinism into the sphere of society is dangerous, as the "social Darwinism" adopted by Hitler's Nazi ideology has shown. It justified the conquest of territories in the name of creating more *Lebensraum* (living space) and the subjugation of other peoples in the name of racial fitness and purity. In our day, the consequences of social Darwinism go beyond armed aggression to the more subtle but in some ways equally merciless struggle of competitors in the marketplace. No-holds-barred competition produces widening gaps between rich and poor and concentrates wealth and power in the hands of corporate managers and international financiers. It relegates states and entire populations to the role of clients and consumers and, if they are poor, dismisses them as marginal factors in the equations that determine success in the global marketplace.

The market distributes benefits. This tenet is directly related to the belief that in the existential struggle only the fittest survive; indeed, it serves as its justification. Unlike in nature, where the consequence of "fitness" is the spread and dominance of a species and the extinction or marginalization of others, in society there is said to be a mechanism that distributes the benefits instead of having them accrue uniquely to the "fit." This is the market, governed by what Adam Smith called the "invisible hand." It acts equitably: if I do well for myself, I benefit not only me, my family, and my company, but also my community. In the economy as a whole, wealth "trickles down" from the rich to the poor. A rising tide, after all, should lift all boats.

The myth of the market is comforting; not surprisingly, it is often cited by those who benefit from it. Unfortunately, it leaves out of account a provision already noted by the classical economists: The market distributes benefits only under conditions of near-perfect competition, where the playing field is level and all players have a more or less equal number of chips. In the real world, the playing field is never level and the distribution of wealth is highly skewed.

Nobody has, or ever had, firsthand experience of the market working equitably for all. In today's world, the market favors the rich at the expense of the poor. Today the wealth of a few hundred billionaires equals the revenue of half the world's peoples, while the poorest 40 percent of humankind is left with three percent of the global wealth.

The more you consume the better you are. This is the belief that there is a strict equivalence between the size of your wallet—as demonstrated, for example, by the size of your car and the size of your house—and your personal worth as the owner of the wallet (and the car and house).

The equating of human worth with financial worth has been consciously fueled by business. In former years, companies did not hesitate to advertise unlimited consumption as a realistic possibility and conspicuous consumption as the ideal. Victor Lebov, a U.S. retailing analyst writing shortly after World War II, put the consumerist philosophy in terms reminiscent of a myth. "Our enormously productive economy," he said, "demands that we make consumption our way of life, that we convert the buying and use of goods into rituals, that we seek our spiritual satisfaction, our ego satisfaction, in consumption. The economy needs things consumed, burned, worn out, replaced, and discarded at an ever-increasing rate" (quoted by Alan Durning in *How Much Is Enough?* Norton, 1992). The consumption myth was, and to some extent still is, extremely powerful. According to some estimates, in constant dollars the modern world has consumed as many goods and services since 1950 as in all previous generations put together.

Not only are there more consumers than ever in the world, but each consumer also consumes more than ever. Since 1960, the proportion of U.S. households with dishwashers rose from 7 percent to 50 percent, the proportion of households with air conditioning went from 15 percent to 73 percent, and car ownership doubled. This trend, evidently, is not sustainable, whether in America or elsewhere. The consequences and side effects of consumerism were not known 50 years ago, but they cannot be ignored today. Overconsumption depletes precious resources and negatively affects both physical health and mental equilibrium and it worsens the structural imbalance in the world economy. Yet the myth that one is a better, indeed a superior, person when one owns more and uses more is persistent. Conspicuous consumption is still an indicator of social status. This is not as frankly admitted today as it was in the past, but in many ways the marketing of houses, cars, and consumer goods is still counting on it—and, it appears, with good reason.

The more money you have, the happier you are. The great majority of people in the industrialized world believe that there is a connection between having money and feeling good. Gallup opinion surveys found that three in four young Americans entering college consider it "essential" or "very important" that they become very well off financially. Asked what makes for a good life, a 1996 Roper poll found that 63 percent of Americans say "a lot of money."

Yet the belief about the connection between wealth and happiness is not borne out by people's experience. If this belief were true, the citizens of rich nations should be happier than those of poor nations. This is not the case. A survey of 43 countries by Ronald Inglehart indicates that once a country reaches the level of about $10,000 GNP per person, increases in the nation's wealth do not produce increases in its inhabitants' sense of well-being. Bulgarians are neither prosperous nor satisfied and Scandinavians and West Germans are more so, but the Irish claim to be just as satisfied as the Germans and the Scandinavians, although they have less than half their GNP. Moreover, rich individuals should be happier than the poor, and the super-rich should be happiest of all. But a *Forbes* survey of the 100 wealthiest Americans showed that millionaires experience only slightly greater happiness than the average individual.

Since 1957, GNP in the United States has more than doubled, but the average level of happiness has declined: those who report being "very happy" are only 32 percent of the population. At the same time the divorce rate doubled, the teen suicide rate more than doubled, violent crime tripled, and more people than ever say they are depressed.

Social psychologist David Myers called this the "syndrome of soaring wealth and shrinking spirit." More than ever, he noted, we have big houses and broken homes, high income and low morale, secured rights and diminished civility. We excel at making a living but fail at making a life.

It appears that money can buy many things but not happiness and well-being. It can buy sex but not love, attention but not caring, information but not wisdom. Although money is needed to cover essential human needs, beyond that there are other factors that make for happiness and the good life—love and caring within the family, intimate friendships and close emotional ties with others in the workplace and the community, a sense of belonging to one's country and culture, work that is meaningful and productive, contact with nature, and leisure activities that engage our skills and interests and give scope to our creativity.

Economic ends justify military means. The ancient Romans had a saying: If you aspire to peace, prepare for war. This matched their conditions and experience. The Romans had a worldwide empire, with rebellious peoples and cultures within and barbarian tribes at the periphery. Maintaining this empire required a constant exercise of military power. Today the nature of power is very different, but the belief about war is much the same.

The violence that followed the Iraq War showed that trying to achieve economic ends by military means is a poor strategy. In the twenty-first-century world, where humanity is more interacting and interdependent than ever before, and where social, economic, and ecological systems are operating at the edge of chaos, war is not the way to achieve peace or any objective, whether political or economic. War is morally indefensible and, as Vietnam, Afghanistan, and Iraq testify, it is seldom justified by its results. It is with good reason that a statement of the Club of Budapest (reproduced in Appendix C) declared, "Given that modern warfare kills innocent civilians, inflicts serious damage on the life-supporting environment, and may escalate to a global conflagration, waging war is a crime against all of humanity. It needs to be recognized as such. No nation-state should have the legitimate right to declare war on any other nation-state."

Shedding today's obsolete beliefs does not mean giving up *all* beliefs. A society's commonly accepted beliefs help explain the world, guide individual and collective aspiration, and provide shared direction. But beliefs can outlive their usefulness, and then they become useless and even dangerous. When that happens, it is in society's interest to shed them. Countless once-functional and flowering beliefs have become obsolete. In Central America, dozens of Mayan temples lie abandoned; in Peru, Incan monuments are scattered in ruins. Celtic cairns in Wales, Khmer statues in Kampuchea, Sumerian ziggurats in Iraq, and giant stone heads on Easter Island are all mute witnesses of once-flowering systems of belief that have disappeared as more potent beliefs appeared in their place.

Adopt a New Morality

In a healthy society, the members share a common morality: They perceive what is right and wrong, good and bad in basically similar ways. Without a shared morality, people cannot readily distinguish between what they should consider right and wrong, moral and immoral. But beyond the borders of a nation and culture, the morality that holds people together fails to provide guidance. What is moral in one culture and society may be unacceptable and perhaps reprehensible in another. The result is international and intercultural tension and conflict.

In an interacting and interdependent world, there is urgent need for a morality that can be accepted by all people, wherever they live. This morality need not flatten the diversity of contemporary peoples and cultures, and it need not place in question their moral sensibilities. A truly universal morality links today's diverse peoples and cultures, based on beliefs and objectives they can share and adopt. It respects people's personal morality and the moral principles of their cultures, but adds to them more-embracing values and principles.

Our *personal* morality varies with the personality, ambitions, and circumstances of each of us. It reflects our unique background, heritage, and family and community situation. Our *cultural* morality selects the values we must share with others if our community is to maintain the level of cohesion it needs for its functioning. This morality matches our community's culture, social structure, economic development, and environment. A *universal* morality adds to these local and regional moralities an international and intercultural dimension. It does not prescribe the nature of individual, national, and cultural morality; it only ensures that these moralities do not give rise to behaviors that are damaging to the global community and its life-supporting environment.

How could a universal morality arise and spread in society? Traditionally, setting the norms of morality was the task of the religions. The Ten Commandments of Jews and Christians, the Provisions for the Faithful in Islam, and the Rules of Right Livelihood of the Buddhists are examples. Today the dominance of science has reduced the power of religious doctrines to regulate human behavior, and many people look to science for practical guidance. Yet classical science could not come up with principles that would provide a basis for universal morality. Saint-Simon in the late 1700s, Auguste Comte in the early 1800s, and Émile Durkheim in the late 1800s and early 1900s tried to develop "positive" scientific observation- and experiment-based principles for a meaningful and publicly acceptable ethic. But this endeavor was so foreign to classical science's commitment to value neutrality that it was not taken up by the great majority of scientists in the twentieth century.

In the 1990s, scientists as well as political leaders began to recognize the need for principles that would state universal norms for behavior. In April 1990, in the "Universal Declaration of Human Responsibilities," the InterAction Council, a group of 24 former heads of state or government declared, "Because global interdependence demands that we must live with each other in harmony, human beings need rules and constraints. Ethics are the minimum standards that make a collective life possible. Without ethics and the resulting self-restraint, humankind would revert to the survival of the fittest. The world is in need of an ethical base on which to stand."

The Union of Concerned Scientists, an organization of leading scientists, concurred. "A new ethic is required," claimed a statement signed in 1993 by

1,670 scientists from 70 countries, including 102 Nobel laureates. "This ethic must motivate a great movement, convincing reluctant leaders and reluctant governments and reluctant peoples themselves to effect the needed changes." The scientists noted our new responsibility for caring for the Earth and warned that "a great change in our stewardship of the Earth and the life on it is required if vast human misery is to be avoided and our global home on this planet is not to be irretrievably mutilated." Human beings and the natural world, they said, are on a collision course. This may so alter the living world that it will be unable to sustain life as we know it.

In November 2003, a group of Nobel Peace laureates meeting in Rome affirmed, "Ethics in the relations between nations and in government policies is of paramount importance. Nations must treat other nations as they wish to be treated. The most powerful nations must remember that as they do, so shall others do." And in November 2004, the same group of laureates declared, "Only by reaffirming our shared ethical values—respect for human rights and fundamental freedoms—and by observing democratic principles, within and amongst countries, can terrorism be defeated. We must address the root causes of terrorism—poverty, ignorance and injustice—rather than responding to violence with violence."

Undoubtedly, the time has come to give serious attention to a morality that can be embraced by all people regardless of their creed, religion, race, sex, or secular belief. It must have intuitive appeal, addressing the basic moral instinct present in all healthy individuals. This merits further thought. Now that the moral prescriptions of Marx, Lenin, and Mao have failed in the practice of communist countries, the most widely espoused morality in the world is liberalism, the conceptual heritage of Bentham, Locke, and Hume of the school of classical British philosophy. People are not to be prevented from pursuing their self-interest as long as they observe the rules that permit life in civilized society. "Live and let live" is the liberal principle. You can live in any way you please, as long as you do not break the law.

In today's world, classical liberalism makes for a misplaced form of tolerance. Letting everyone live as they please as long as they keep within the law entails a serious risk. The rich and the powerful could (and do) consume a disproportionate share of the resources to which the poor, too, have a legitimate claim, and both rich and poor could (and do) inflict irreversible damage on the environment that all people must share.

Rather than "live and let live," we need a universal morality just as intuitively meaningful and instinctively appealing as liberalism, but better adapted to the conditions in which humankind now finds itself. Such a morality substitutes for liberalism's "Live and let live" Gandhi's "Live more simply, so others can simply live."

Following Gandhi's advice is even more urgent today than it was in his day. It is also easier to do. Today we realize that living simply is not a comedown. On the contrary, simple living is the fruit of a free choice that makes for greater personal well-being and a deeper sense of meaning in life. It is living in a way that is socially and ecologically sustainable and thus responsible to all things on Earth today and for generations to come.

Of course, the key consideration is not the intrinsic simplicity of our lifestyle, but the impact of our life on society and nature. This impact must not exceed the capacity of the planet to provide for the basic needs of all its people. Hence the indicated principle of universal morality is *Live in a way that allows all other people to live as well.*

The shift toward a universal morality is slow in coming; the initially noble but now outdated precept "live and let live" persists. Yet if all people used and overused private cars, smoked, ate a diet heavy in meat, and made use of the myriad appliances that go with the affluent lifestyle, the essential resources of the planet would be rapidly exhausted and its self-generative powers would be drastically reduced.

If the Chinese, the Indian, the African, the Latin American, and other developing country populations were to continue to burn coal for electricity and wood for cooking, abide by classical economic policies, and acquire Western living, driving, and consumer habits, planetary limits would also be overstepped. Only if both rich and poor embrace a universal morality is there a chance of entering on a positive path to our shared future.

Thomas Jefferson said that if you believe that the people are not sufficiently informed to exercise power in society, the democratic solution is not to take power from their hands but to inform them. This is not a quixotic endeavor. If people realize that a universal principle of morality is needed to ensure humanity's survival, and that abiding by it does not call for unreasonable sacrifices, they will respond.

The need for a universal morality is real, and it can be made evident. The survival of humanity is intimately tied to solidarity and cooperation in the global community and respect for the integrity of nature. If we continue to act as we do now, the current decision-window will take us to a Chaos Point where our systems tip to a devolutionary path. Societies will be rocked by terrorism and crime, international relations will be rent by wars and intolerance, and the biosphere will turn inhospitable for human life and habitation, with eroding agricultural lands, hostile weather patterns, rising sea levels, and the proliferation of microorganisms incompatible with our species.

We can also make clear that abiding by a universal morality does not entail undue sacrifice. Living in a way that enables all others to live as well does not mean being self-denying: We can continue to strive for excellence and beauty, personal growth and enjoyment, even for comfort and luxury. But when we are guided by universal moral principles, we define the pleasures and achievements of life in relation to the quality of enjoyment and level of satisfaction they provide, rather than in terms of the amount of money they cost and the quantity of materials and energy their production and use call for.

Dream Your World and Act on It

In 1968, when Robert Kennedy was running for the presidential nomination, he said, "Some men see things as they are and say, *why*; I dream things that never were and say, *why not*." To dream the world as you wish to see it is never just to indulge an idle fancy. Today, living in a window in time that decides our future, it has more relevance than ever.

A Tale from Arabian Nights

The power of a vision of the world as we dream it is illustrated in the following tale:

In ancient Arabia, Mamun son of Harun al Rashid, inherited a city. When he came to take possession, he found it in disorder and on the verge of ruin. Persian traders, falling into dispute with the citizens in the markets, had found them weak and had become emboldened to pillage and violence.

The young prince was advised to set forth a new code of law and enforce it. This he did; but with the result that disputes multiplied, the citizens were impoverished, and traders began to avoid the city. In despair Mamun bethought himself of a device. He secretly brought together certain foreign craftsmen, and enjoined them to work out in ivory and precious woods the image of a surpassingly beautiful city, whose design he gave to them. When it was finished, he rewarded them richly and sent them away; and bore the image by night to the chief mosque, concealing it behind a curtain.

Mamun then issued an edict that every traveler and trader entering the gates must first be brought to this mosque to worship, and be pledged to silence. The image was there revealed to them; and it became evident to the citizens by the altered demeanor of these strangers that they had seen a noble vision of which they could not or dared not speak. They demanded to see it also—which was what Mamun had desired: they were accordingly admitted, one by one, on the same conditions.

Now it began to appear that the ruler of the artists was more successful than the ruler of the lawmakers; for, changed by the sight of the image, the people carried out their business in peace. Order, gaiety, and wealth returned silently to the place. And in its rebuilding, the city which Mamun inherited resembled the city of his dream.

In our day we do not need to build the image of a peaceful and orderly city in ivory and precious stones; it is enough that we dream it, making our vision as concrete as we can. In chapter 5 we have already attempted to "dream" the nature of a peaceful and sustainable civilization. Dreams that envision the longer-term future and the entire human family can be brought down to the here and now. This is a task that only you and others like you can perform. You should use your creativity and imagination and ask: This is how things *could* be—why are they not like that? For example, what is keeping your neighborhood, city, town, or village from being a place

- that is safe for everyone to live and work and for children to grow up, and where community services and public transportation are available to all;
- where nobody is marginalized, hopelessly hungry and unemployed, and without a voice in running the community and deciding its future;
- where government representatives and town officials are honest and informed, and represent the best interests of all people in the community;
- where the schools and hospitals are clean, well-staffed, competent, and capable of serving the needs of the community;
- where the air is breathable, the rivers and lakes unpolluted, parks well kept, and a more pristine nature can be enjoyed by everyone;

- where the inhabitants are selective about how they consume and what they discard, throw waste into the right bins, and pick up after their dog on the street;
- and where people have time to greet each other, inquire about the each other's needs and well-being, and do their jobs courteously?

When you see things as they are and ask *why are things the way they are—* which is likely to be very different from the way you dream it—you come across a maze of complex explanations and a tangle of unsolved problems. But if you dare to dream, and share your dream with friends and neighbors and ask, *why are things not the way I dream it,* you will find answers—and ways you can come together to start making a world that resembles your dream.

Evolve Your Consciousness

Margaret Mead said, "Never doubt the power of a small group of people to change the world. Nothing else ever has." Mahatma Gandhi was even more insistent: *"Be* the change you want to see in the world." They were right. When you evolve your consciousness, you have the power to change the world.

Why is consciousness so potent? The explanation is at hand: In a decision-window, even small "fluctuations" can change the destiny of the system. A fluctuation in the form of a more evolved consciousness is particularly powerful. A more evolved consciousness means new thinking, and it is the key to a new civilization. A new civilization, in turn, is the key to the well-being, and even the survival, of humankind.

We know that when a living species is threatened with extinction, it faces a stark choice: It either produces a viable mutation or it becomes extinct. For the species to survive, the way its members maintain themselves in their environment and the way they reproduce have to change. In nonhuman species, most behavior concerned with survival is genetically coded, and changing it calls for an adaptive mutation of the gene pool. Genetic mutation is slow, but it can work: The fit mutants reproduce and become dominant, and the unfit are eliminated by natural selection.

In regard to human society, the situation is not quite the same. When the survival of a population, culture, or civilization is threatened, if it is not to face extinction it too must produce a viable change in the way its members live and reproduce. But this does not require a mutation of the gene pool. While some aspects of our behavior are genetically coded, the values and beliefs that threaten our survival are influenced mainly by our culture. Society is culturally and not genetically coded, and our culture is more flexible than our genes: We can mutate it if we wish, whereas we cannot change our gene pool. A cultural mutation can be willfully launched and consciously oriented. The conscious orientation of the next cultural mutation—the shift to a new civilization—depends on the evolution of our consciousness. This evolution has become a precondition of our collective survival.

You can help humanity survive; you can evolve your consciousness. One way you can do this is by entering a so-called ASC: an altered state of consciousness. Our ordinary wakeful consciousness is but one of many kinds of consciousness we possess and many states of consciousness we can enter. Entering the altered states of consciousness that are typical of deep meditation and intense prayer is particularly important. It allows you to experience a profound oneness with others around you, as well as with nature. In traditional cultures, ASCs were regularly experienced: They were highly valued and fostered by repeated rituals. They are accessible to modern people as well. Psychiatrist Stanislav Grof, who induced such states in thousands of patients, found that even highly trained psychologists, when they have experiences of altered states, shift to a consciousness that places the mechanistic, materialistic, and fragmented worldview of the modern age in the context of a holistic and embracing vision.

Astronauts traveling in space and viewing the Earth in its living splendor also experience an altered state of consciousness; and they, too, feel an intense tie to their home planet, a feeling that persists for the rest of their days. People who have come close to death in an accident or illness come back from this altered-state experience and see life in a new way. They have a fresh appreciation of existence and reverence for nature; they evolve deep humanitarian and ecological concerns and find differences among people, whether in the area of sex, race, color, language, political conviction, or religious belief, interesting and enriching rather than threatening.

People who have experienced a deeply altered state of consciousness realize that they cannot do anything to nature without simultaneously doing it to themselves, and that other people—whether next door, in distant parts of the world, or of generations yet to come—are not separate from them and their fate is not a matter of indifference.

Not everybody can be expected to engage in deep prayer or meditation, undergo treatment by transpersonal psychiatrists, have near-death experiences, or be shot into space, yet a more evolved consciousness is needed in everyone.

Fortunately, there are also more accessible paths leading to it. You can train your inner self to become more one with your outer self, achieving greater unity between body and mind. When you become whole, you can begin to make the world around you whole.

How can you become whole? We need to start with ourselves. In the ever-increasing stress of everyday life, we are losing touch with ourselves, with nature, and with what is truly important in life. This is a long-standing problem in the modern world. In an essay written 150 years ago, entitled "Life without Principle," Henry David Thoreau asked that we take the time to consider the way in which we spend our lives. This world, he said, is a place of business. If a man was tossed out of a window when an infant and made a cripple for life, he is regretted chiefly because he is incapacitated for business. "If a man walks in the woods for love of them half of each day, he is in danger of being regarded as a loafer; but if he spends his whole day as a speculator, shearing off those woods and making earth bald before her time, he is esteemed as an industrious and enterprising citizen." There is nothing, said Thoreau, not even crime, more opposed to life itself than this incessant business.

Thoreau noted that when our life ceases to be inward and private, conversation degenerates into mere gossip. We rarely meet a man, he said, who can tell us any news which he has not read in a newspaper or been told by a neighbor. In proportion as our inward life fails, we go more constantly and desperately to the post office. "The poor fellow who walks away with the greatest number of letters, proud of his extensive correspondence, has not heard from himself in a long while." We could say much the same today, and we do not even need to go to the post office. We merely turn on our computer.

Thoreau admitted to being more than usually jealous of his freedom. Those slight obligations that afforded him a livelihood were as yet a pleasure to him and he was not often reminded that they were a necessity. But he could foresee that if his wants should be much increased, the labor required to supply them would become a drudgery. And then, said Thoreau, there would be nothing left worth living for . . .

In our day, we cannot extricate ourselves from the "bustle of incessant business," as Thoreau did later, living for two years in a cabin in the woods, but we can reserve a few hours, and an occasional day, for getting in touch with ourselves, with nature, and with those around us. This is a first and vital step on the way to inner growth. When you take it, you are already on the way to evolving your consciousness.

Another step you can take is to get in touch with your body. We use our body as we use our car or computer: giving it commands to take us where we want to go and do what we want to have done. We live in our head, with little time and inclination to live in our whole body. We are losing the ground under our feet.

Sophisticated methods can help you to ground yourself. They include traditional ways such as tai chi, qi gong, yoga, and Ayurvedic and other holistic methods and exercises, as well as new and old breathing techniques and techniques of deep relaxation. Even a simple exercise, practiced regularly, can help you achieve contact with your body. *Sit for a few minutes comfortably relaxed, with hands on knees and eyes closed. Concentrate on your body and feel it bit by bit, starting with the tips of your toes and ending with the top of your head. Become aware of your breathing—feel how every breath you take penetrates your lungs and makes energy course through your veins. Feel the rhythms of your body—the subtle movement of the muscles, the beating of the heart, and the working of the organs.* Soon you will begin to feel your whole body and begin to feel at home in it. You will recover some of the sense of wholeness modern people have lost in the stress and strain of everyday existence.

The stresses and strains of existence also have an impact on our emotional life, and that, too, needs attention. It is not that we have lost contact with our emotions—we are only too aware of them most of the time. Only, they are often the wrong kind of emotions. Negative feelings such as anger, hate, fear, anxiety, suspicion, jealousy, contempt, and indifference dominate the tenor of modern existence. They result from lifetime experiences that are mainly negative. With some exceptions, even childhood education is based on negative reinforcements such as punishment and the threat of failure. Positive emotions of love and caring are the preserve of the family and circle of friends, but these aspects of life are frequently sacrificed to pressure of work and the strain of securing one's daily existence.

Positive emotions can also be generated by intimate experiences of nature: beholding the tranquility of a sunny meadow or a calm lake, the beauty of a sunset, the majesty of a mountain, and the awesomeness of a stormy sea. But for big-city people, these experiences are few and far between. Even when they are accessible, as in hiking, biking, or on the golf course, they are often subordinated to the pursuit of professional goals and social aspirations, such as winning over a client, or impressing a friend or neighbor with one's conversation or the latest fashion.

A vicious cycle holds most of us in its grip: Negative experiences generate negative attitudes that create further negative experiences. This cycle must be broken. You need to take stock of your feelings and make a conscious effort to transform negative emotions. It is not easy to replace hate with love, suspicion with trust, contempt with respect, jealousy with appreciation, and anxiety with self-assurance, yet it can be done. All the religions and spiritual traditions of the world offer ways to do it. There are also secular techniques. Group experiences allow you to share your fears and hopes as do diverse psychotherapies, including reliving the experiences of our childhood, infancy, birth, and even our time in the womb.

If you make a sincere attempt at emotional purification, the vicious cycle of negative experiences generating further negative experiences will be replaced by a virtuous cycle of positive feelings toward others, generating understanding and empathy in family, friends, collaborators, and the community.

Recovering your ties with others and with nature, integrating your mind and body, and transforming your emotions are *ends* as well as *means*. They are valuable in themselves and also serve as steps on the road to further growth. When you are grounded in your body and centered in your emotions, when you are in touch with nature and with others around you, you can open your body-mind to the world and become a positive part of its transformation.

Ten Benchmarks of an Evolved Consciousness

You possess a more evolved consciousness when you:

1. Live in ways that enable all other people to live as well, satisfying your needs without detracting from the chances of other people to satisfy theirs.

2. Live in ways that respect the right to life and to economic and cultural development of all people, wherever they live and whatever their ethnic origin, sex, citizenship, station in life, and belief system.

3. Live in ways that safeguard the intrinsic right to life and to an environment supportive of life for all the things that live and grow on Earth.

4. Pursue happiness, freedom, and personal fulfillment in harmony with the integrity of nature and with consideration for the similar pursuits of others in society.

5. Require that your government relate to other nations and peoples peacefully and in a spirit of cooperation, recognizing the legitimate aspirations for a better life and a healthy environment of all the people in the human family.

6. Require business enterprises to accept responsibility for all their stakeholders as well as for the sustainability of their environment,

demanding that they produce goods and offer services that satisfy legitimate demand without impairing nature and reducing the opportunities of smaller and less privileged entrants to compete in the marketplace.

7. Require public media to provide a constant stream of reliable information on basic trends and crucial processes to enable you and other citizens and consumers to reach informed decisions on issues that affect your and their life and well-being.

8. Make room in your life to help those less privileged than you to live a life of dignity, free from the struggles and humiliations of abject poverty.

9. Encourage young people and open-minded people of all ages to evolve the spirit that could empower them to make ethical decisions of their own on issues that decide their future and the future of their children.

10. Work with like-minded people to preserve or restore the essential balances of the environment, with attention to your neighborhood, your country or region, and the whole of the biosphere.

Addressing a joint session of the U.S. Congress in February of 1991, Václav Havel, then the president of Czechoslovakia, said, "Without a global revolution in the sphere of human consciousness, nothing will change for the better . . . and the catastrophe towards which this world is headed—the ecological, social, demographic, or general breakdown of civilization—will be unavoidable." Havel's point is well taken, but it is not a reason for pessimism: The breakdown of civilization can be avoided. Human consciousness can evolve. It is already evolving, and you can help it evolve further.

Former U.S. president Harry Truman remarked in turn, "The buck stops here," meaning the desk at the Oval Office. Today the buck is more democratic: It stops not only in the White House, but with you and me, and everyone around us. It comes in the form of a challenge: Reexamine your thinking, evolve your consciousness. If you do so, the brave but as yet insufficiently powerful and organized movement toward a more holistic, peaceful, and sustainable civilization could turn into a groundswell that does away with the mindset that generated our problems, and orients you and those around you toward a world you can live in, and can leave with good conscience to your children.

We are the music makers,
And we are the dreamers of dreams,

Wandering by lone seabreakers,
And sitting by desolate streams;
World-losers and world-forsakers,
On whom the pale moon gleams:
Yet we are the movers and shakers
Of the world forever, it seems . . .
We, in the ages lying
In the buried past of the earth,
Built Ninevah with our sighing,
And Babel itself in our mirth;
And o'erthrew them with prophesying
To the old of the new world's worth;
For each age is a dream that is dying,
Or one that is coming to birth.

—Arthur O'Shaughnessy

The Scientific Background

The Emerging Holism of the Sciences

The main features of the holism emerging today in the principal branches of the empirical sciences are an important and hopeful development; they deserve closer acquaintance.

Holism in the New Physics

Classical physics was mechanistic and reductionist; it reposed on Newton's uncontested laws of nature, published in his *Philosophiae Naturalis Principia Mathematica* (Mathematical Principles of Natural Philosophy) in 1687. These laws and the system in which they are stated became the foundation of modern-age Logos, the mechanistic worldview that achieved its fullest expression in the industrial civilization of the twentieth century. They demonstrated with geometrical certainty that material bodies on Earth are made up of mass points and move according to mathematically expressible rules, while planets rotate in accordance with Kepler's laws in the heavens. They showed that the motion of all masses is fully determined by the conditions under which motion is initiated, just as the motion of a pendulum is determined by its length and its initial displacement and the motion of a projectile is determined by its launch angle and acceleration. But classical physics is not the physics of our day. Although Newtonian laws apply to objects moving at modest speeds on the surface of the Earth, the conceptual framework in which these motions are embedded has shifted radically.

The classical view of nature began to crumble at the end of the nineteenth century, when the basic building blocks of the universe turned out not to be basic after all. The supposedly indivisible atom, of which all things in the world were said to be constructed, proved fissionable into a bewildering variety of components. The "elementary" particles themselves dissolved in a swirl of energy. Max Planck discovered that light, like all energy, comes not in a continuous stream but in discrete packets called quanta; Michael Faraday and James Clerk Maxwell came up with theories of nonmaterial phenomena such as electromagnetic fields; and Einstein advanced the special and the general theories of relativity.

The death knell of the classical concepts was sounded in the 1920s with the advent of quantum mechanics, the physics of the ultrasmall domains of reality. The packets of bound energy known as "quanta" refused to behave like commonsense objects. Their behavior proved to be more and more weird. Einstein, who received the Nobel Prize for his work on the photoelectric effect (in which streams of light quanta are generated on irradiated plates), did not suspect, and was never ready to accept, the weirdness of the quantum world. But physicists investigating the behavior of the particles that carry light, matter, and force found that, until registered by an instrument of detection or another act of observation, these particles have no specific position, nor do they occupy a unique state. It appears that the ultimate units of physical reality have no uniquely determinable location, and they exist in a superposition of several potential states at the same time.

Perhaps the most remarkable feature of quanta is their subtle but constant and apparently space- and time-transcending interconnection. The fundamental units of the physical world prove to be intrinsically and instantly "entangled" with each other.

The concept of entanglement was put forward by Erwin Schrödinger in the 1930s, and since then a large number of controlled experiments have testified to its reality. It turns out that once two or more quanta enter the same state, they remain instantly linked no matter how far they may be from each other. This strange space- and time-transcending connection came to light when a thought experiment proposed by Einstein with colleagues Boris Podolsky and Nathan Rosen (the so-called "EPR experiment") was tested by physical instrumentation. The pathbreaking experiment was performed by French physicist Alain Aspect in the 1980s and has since been replicated in laboratories in many parts of the world. It is important enough to merit more detailed description.

Einstein proposed the experiment in the expectation that it would overcome the limitation on measuring the various states of a particle simultaneously (known as the Heisenberg "principle of uncertainty"). The idea is to take two particles in a so-called singlet state, where their spins cancel out each other to yield a total spin of zero. We then allow the particles to separate and travel a finite distance. By measuring the spin states of both particles, we overcome the principle of uncertainty, for we get a reading of both spin states at the same time.

When this experiment is carried out, a strange thing takes place: No matter how far the twin particles are separated, when one measures one of them, the measurement on the other corresponds precisely to the results of the measurement on the first—even though this result was not, and could not have been, determined in advance. It is as if the second particle "knows" what is happening to the first. The information that underlies this strange knowledge appears to be conveyed over any finite distance, and to be conveyed nearly instantly. In Aspect's experiments, the speed of its transmission was estimated to be about 20 times faster than the velocity of light; and in a subsequent experiment performed by Nicolas Gisin, it proved to be 20,000 times faster than this supposedly insuperable speed barrier.

Recently a number of widely reported "teleportation experiments" have shown that entire atoms, not only quanta, can be entangled. In the spring of 2004, two teams of physicists, one at the National Institute of Standards in Colorado and the other at the University of Innsbruck in Austria, demonstrated that the quantum state of entire atoms can be teleported by transporting the quantum bits ("qubits") that define the entangled atoms. In Austria, qubits are routinely teleported from one side of the Danube to another, a distance of about 700 meters.

The world of the new physics may be strange, but it is not incomprehensible. Its relevant feature is time- and space-transcending entanglement: the kind of instant interconnection called *nonlocality*. The new physics has accepted the fact that all quanta in the universe, most directly those that share or have ever shared the same quantum state, remain intrinsically connected with each other. This is both a microphysical and a cosmological phenomenon. It involves the very smallest as well as the very largest structures of the universe.

Nonlocality tells us that all things in the world are interconnected, and all are part of more integrated ensembles: wholes. This is the essence of the holism of the new physics. As quantum theorist Henry Stapp declared, it is possibly the most profound discovery in all of science. Not only are the ultrasmall domains of reality nonlocal, but so are the superlarge domains. Cosmologists Menas Kafatos and Robert Nadeau entitled their study of the cosmos *The Non-Local Universe,* and physicist Chris Clarke affirmed that the whole universe is an entangled quantum system.

Holism in the New Biology

For the better part of the past two centuries, biology was beset by speculative, so-called metaphysical elements. Some biologists championed vitalism (the concept that life is infused with a vital force or energy); others opted for teleology (the notion that life and evolution tend toward a predetermined goal or "telos"). Reacting against these nineteenth-century ideas, twentieth-century life scientists turned to the contrary approach, which was to emulate classical physics in viewing the organism as a complex mechanism. They assumed that the organism can be understood as a collection of interacting parts, such as cells, organs, or organ systems. The parts can be analyzed individually, and this analysis can show how their interaction produces the functions and manifestations of the processes of life.

The analytic approach gave rise to molecular biology and modern genetics and encouraged the current trend toward genetic engineering. The initial success of these technologies seemed to provide sufficient proof of the correctness of the molecular approach, and it became accepted as the paradigm in the life sciences.

In the late twentieth century, however, the mechanistic conception of life became increasingly questioned. Leading biologists pointed out that the alternative to mechanism is not a return to vitalism and teleology, but the organismic approach. This was explored as a philosophy by the great process thinkers of the late nineteenth and early twentieth centuries, notably Henri Bergson, Samuel Alexander, Lloyd Morgan, and Alfred North Whitehead. The latter's concept of the organism as a fundamental metaphor for all things in the physical and living realms served as a rallying point for the post-Darwinian developmental schools, the avant-garde of the new biology.

The developmental approach maintains that the organism has a level and form of integrity that cannot be fully understood merely by studying its parts in interaction. The concept "the whole is more than the sum of its parts" holds, for when the parts are integrated within the living organism, properties emerge and processes take place that are not the simple sum of the properties of the parts. The living organism cannot be reduced to the interaction of its parts without losing its "emergent properties"—the very characteristics that make it living.

Coherence is the concept that best expresses the wholeness that is currently being discovered in the realms of life. An organically coherent system is integrated and dynamic, its myriad activities self-motivated, self-organizing, and spontaneous, engaging all levels simultaneously from the microscopic and molecular all the way to the macroscopic. The constant communication of all parts in the organism allows adjustments, responses, and changes required for the maintenance of the whole system to propagate in all directions at once.

For the understanding of the nature of organic coherence, biophysicist Mae-Wan Ho suggested that a dance group or jazz band is a good example. In such an ensemble, the performers are perfectly in tune with each other, and even the audience becomes one with the dance and the music. The "song and dance" within the living organism ranges over more than 70 octaves, with localized chemical bonds vibrating, molecular wheels turning, microcilia beating, fluxes of electrons and protons propagating, and metabolites and ionic currents within and among cells flowing through ten orders of spatial magnitude.

Similarly to nonlocality at the ultrasmall scale of the physical world, there are intrinsic and quasi-instant connections and correlations in the world of life. These allow changes to propagate throughout the organism, making even distant sites neighboring. This is a major change in regard to the mechanistic concept that considers that the parts of the organism are distinct entities with definite boundaries in space and time.

Coherence in the living realm ranges from the smallest element in an organism to the full range of life on the planet. It encompasses multienzyme complexes inside cells, the organization of cells into tissues and organs, the polymorphism of living species within ecological communities, and the entire web of life in the biosphere.

If the living world is a subtly but effectively interconnected whole, it is not the harsh domain of classical Darwinism, where chance rules the evolution of species, and where each organism struggles for fitness and survival against all. Rather, the entire web of life is a coherent system that evolves through what biologist Brian Goodwin calls the "sacred dance" of the organism with its milieu. Subtle strains of that dance extend to all the species and ecologies in the biosphere.

Holism in the New Psychology

Since the first half of the twentieth century, Gestalt psychology has insisted on the wholeness of the human mind. Gestalt psychologists have shown that the mind strives toward wholeness in all its operations, seeking closure and completion even in ordinary perception. But the wholeness currently discovered in the newest branches of psychology goes considerably beyond this. It shows that the entire sphere of mind and consciousness forms a subtly but effectively interconnected whole. This is a radical departure from the classical theories.

In the classical view, our picture of the world is assembled on the basis of sensory perceptions. It is said that everything that is in the mind must have first been in the eye. Today leading psychologists, psychiatrists, and consciousness researchers are rediscovering that this is not entirely true. At times, our consciousness is informed by nonsensory, so-called transpersonal elements as well.

Psychology and parapsychology laboratories produce impressive evidence that transpersonal forms of information reach the human mind. The evidence comes from controlled experiments, in which explanations in terms of hidden sensory cues, machine bias, cheating by subjects, and experimenter incompetence or error were found unable to account for a number of statistically significant unexpected, so-called paranormal results.

In the early 1970s, physicists Russell Targ and Harold Puthoff undertook a series of tests on thought and image transference. They placed the "receiver" in a sealed, opaque, and electrically shielded chamber, and the "sender" in another room where he or she was subjected to bright flashes of light at regular intervals. The brain-wave patterns of both sender and receiver were registered on electroencephalograph (EEG) machines. As expected, the sender exhibited the rhythmic brain waves that normally accompany exposure to bright flashes of light. After a brief interval, however, the receiver also began to produce the same patterns, although the receiver was not being directly exposed to the flashes and was not receiving sense-perceivable signals from the sender.

Targ and Puthoff also conducted experiments on remote viewing. In these tests, sender and receiver were separated by distances that precluded any form of sensory communication between them. At a site chosen at random, the sender acted as a "beacon," and the receiver tried to pick up what the sender saw. To document their impressions, receivers gave verbal descriptions, usually accompanied by sketches. Independent judges found that the descriptions and the sketches matched the characteristics of the site seen by the sender an average of 66 percent of the time.

Other remote-viewing experiments involved various distances, ranging from half a mile to several thousand miles. Regardless of where they were carried out and by whom, the success rate proved to be well above random probability. The most successful viewers are those who are relaxed, attentive, and meditative. They report receiving a preliminary impression as a gentle and fleeting form that gradually evolves into an integrated image. They initially experience the image as a surprise, both because it is clear and because it is clearly elsewhere.

In addition to images, a variety of physiological effects seem likewise available for nonsensory transmission. Effects of this kind came to be known as *telesomatic*: they consist of changes triggered in the body of a targeted person by the mental processes of another.

Telesomatic effects recall the processes anthropologists call "sympathetic magic." Shamans, witch doctors, and other practitioners of sympathetic magic act not on the person they target but on an effigy of that person, such as a doll. This practice is widespread among traditional peoples, including Native Americans. In his famous work *The Golden Bough,* Sir James Frazer noted that Native American shamans would model the figure of a person in clay and then prick it with a sharp stick or do it some other injury. The corresponding injury was believed to be inflicted on the person the figure represented. Observers found that the targeted person often fell ill, became lethargic, and would sometimes die. Dean Radin and his collaborators at the University of Nevada decided to test the positive variant of this telesomatic effect under controlled laboratory conditions.

In Radin's experiments, the subjects created a small doll in their own image and provided various objects (pictures, jewelry, an autobiography, and personally meaningful tokens) to "represent" them. They also gave a list of what makes them feel nurtured and comfortable. These and the accompanying information were used by the "healers" (who functioned analogously to the "senders" in thought- and image-transfer experiments) to create a sympathetic connection to the subjects (the "patients"). The patients were wired up to monitor the activity of their autonomous nervous system—electrodermal activity, heart rate, blood pulse volume. The healers were in an acoustically and electromagnetically shielded room in an adjacent building. The healers placed the doll and other small objects on the table in front of them and concentrated on them while sending randomly sequenced "nurturing" (active healing) and "rest" messages.

It turned out that the electrodermal activity and heart rates of the patients were significantly different during the active nurturing periods than during the rest periods, and blood pulse volume was significant for a few seconds during the nurturing periods. Both heart rate and blood flow indicated a "relaxation response," which makes sense because the healer was attempting to "nurture" the subject via the doll. On the other hand, a higher rate of electrodermal activity showed that the patient's autonomic nervous system was becoming aroused. Why this should be so was puzzling until the experimenters realized that the healers nurtured the patients by rubbing the shoulders of the dolls that represented them, or stroking the doll's hair and face. This, apparently, had the effect of a "remote massage" on the patients.

Radin and colleagues concluded that the actions and intentions of the healer are mimicked in the patient almost as if they were next to each other. As in other transpersonal experiments, distance between sender and receiver makes little difference. This was confirmed in a large number of experiments by parapsychologists William Braud and Marilyn Schlitz. They found that the mental images of the sender could "reach out over space" to cause changes in the distant receiver. The effects are comparable to those that one's own mental processes produce on one's body. "Telesomatic" action by a distant person is nearly as effective as "psychosomatic" action by the subject on himself or herself.

Further evidence comes from clinical records in hospitals. At the request of patients, "spiritual healers" have been allowed into British National Health Service hospitals since 1970, and are paid by the health service. Psychiatrist Daniel Benor, founder of the United Kingdom's Doctor-Healer Network, examined the records of more than 200 controlled trials of spiritual healing, mainly of humans, but some directed at animals, plants, bacteria, yeasts, laboratory cell cultures, and enzymes. Nearly half had clearly documented effects. Rigorous studies on proximal as well as distant healing at American and European medical schools, hospitals, and experimental laboratories testify that telesomatic effects have notable healing potential.

This writer's experience with psychologist and natural healer Mária Sági, founder of the Koerbler Institute in Budapest, and with physician Gordon Flint, then head of the British Psionic Medical Society, supports Benor's finding. In the past two decades, the writer has been repeatedly diagnosed by the remote method invented independently by Dr. Sági based on the work of Austrian subtle-energy researcher Erich Koerbler, and fifty years previously by the English surgeon George Laurence, founder of the Psionic Medical Society. The diagnoses by Sági and Flint were often carried out over considerable distances: Flint was in Scotland, Sagi in Hungary, and the writer in Tuscany, Italy. Nonetheless, the diagnoses proved accurate and the prescribed homeopathic remedies effective.

This kind of "nonlocal" healing, even though as yet not as widely tested as conventional medicine, is proving its mettle. It is with good reason that American physician Larry Dossey claimed that we have entered a new era in medical practice, Era III, nonlocal medicine. It follows Era II, mind-body medicine, and Era I, standard biochemical medicine.

Our mind seems to be subtly but effectively connected with other minds and other bodies. The renowned psychologist Carl Jung, fascinated with this mysterious aspect of the psyche, theorized that a higher or deeper reality links human minds. He compared unconscious processes in individuals with the myths, legends, and folktales of a variety of cultures at different periods of history and found that the individual records and the collective material contain common themes. This prompted him to postulate a collective aspect of the psyche: the "collective unconscious." He called the dynamic principles that recur in this species-wide memory bank and organize its contents "archetypes."

Jung formulated his concept of archetypes in collaboration with physicist Wolfgang Pauli. They were struck by the fact that while Jung's research into the human psyche led to an encounter with such "irrepresentables" as archetypes, Pauli's research in quantum physics likewise led to "irrepresentables"—the microparticles of the universe, entities for which no complete description appears possible. Jung concluded, "When the existence of two or more irrepresentables is assumed, there is always the possibility—which we tend to overlook—that it may not be a question of two or more factors but of one only." This common factor Jung named *"unus mundus."* In itself, the *unus mundus* is neither psychic nor physical; it stands above, or lies beyond, both *psyche* and *physis.*

If Jung is right, our mind is rooted in a deeper reality. Not everything that appears in our consciousness comes from our senses, and not everything is determined by our own subconscious.

Even if not many people know it yet, the views of the world inspired by Newton, Darwin, and Freud have been overtaken by new discoveries. In light of the emerging conceptions, the universe is not a lifeless, soulless aggregate of inert chunks of matter; rather, it resembles a living organism. Life is not a random accident, and the basic drives of the human psyche include far more than the drive for sex and self-gratification. Matter, life, and mind are consistent elements within an overall process of great complexity yet coherent and harmonious design. Space and time are united as the dynamic background of the observable universe. Matter is vanishing as a fundamental feature of reality, retreating before energy; and continuous fields are replacing discrete particles as the basic elements of an energy-bathed universe. The universe is a seamless whole, evolving over eons of cosmic time and producing conditions in which life, and then mind and consciousness, can emerge.

In the twenty-first century, science is evolving a holistic picture of reality. The emerging holism of the new physics, the new biology, and the newest branches of psychology mesh with and lend fresh legitimacy to the holistic world-concept of the great cultural traditions. The holism of the new civilization we need can have both a scientific and a cultural foundation.

The Chaos Point in the Systems Perspective

Ten Graphics to Help Us Understand Where We Are, and How We Got Here

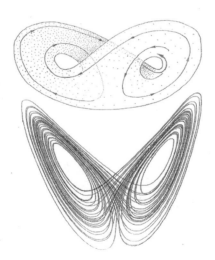

A dynamic system, whether it comes about in nature, in society, or in a computer simulation, is governed by *attractors*. These define the system's "phase portrait": the way it behaves over time. Stable attractors pull the trajectory of the system's development into a recurring and recognizable pattern, either converging on a given point (if governed by point-attractors) or cycling through different states (when under the command of periodic attractors). Dynamic systems, however, can also reach a state where attractors emerge that are not stable, but "strange." These are the chaotic attractors. The first such attractor to be discovered was the "butterfly attractor." It got its name from the shape of the evolutionary path of the global weather system as mapped by meteorologist Edward Lorenz in the 1960s. (In the previous graphic, Lorenz's original model is on the top; a more recent computer-projection is shown below it.)

A complex path of evolution could also characterize more stable systems, but in a chaotic system, a different dynamic comes into play. A system characterized by chaos has a finely structured order, and the smallest "push" or "fluctuation" can impel its development into a different trajectory; this is why the evolution of the world's weather is nearly unpredictable over more extended periods. In a system governed by a chaotic butterfly attractor, even immeasurably small perturbations can shift the evolutionary trajectory from a cycle fluctuating around one of the "wings" to the cycle clumped around the opposite "wing."

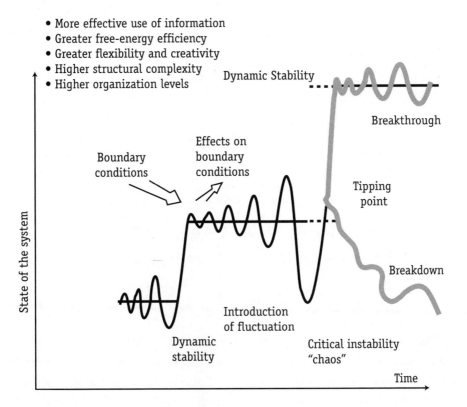

Systems enter a state of chaos when fluctuations that were until then corrected by self-stabilizing negative feedbacks run out of control. The developmental trajectory becomes nonlinear: Prevailing trends break down and in their place come a variety of complex developments. Chaos is seldom a prolonged condition; in most cases, it is but a transitory epoch between more stable states. When fluctuations in the system reach levels of irreversibility, the system reaches a critical point where it either collapses into its individually stable components *(breakdown),* or undergoes rapid evolution toward a state that is resistant to the fluctuations that had destabilized it *(breakthrough).* If the breakthrough path is selected, the system evolves into a state in which it has enhanced information-processing capacity and greater efficiency in the use of free energy, as well as more flexibility, higher structural complexity, and additional levels of organization.

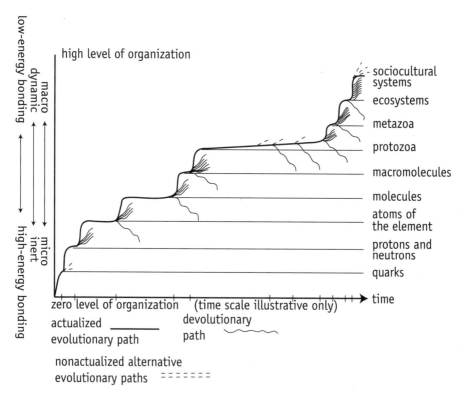

The alternation of periods of dynamic stability and critical instability is typical of evolution throughout nature. It produces a progressive buildup of complexity, from the physical substratum of quarks and elementary particles, through the atoms of the elements, to the molecules formed by atoms and, in a suitable planetary environment, to the macromolecules and cells formed by molecules. On Earth, the progressive buildup of complexity has led to biological systems based on macromolecular and cellular components, further to ecosystems formed by biological systems, and finally to sociocultural systems formed by humans.

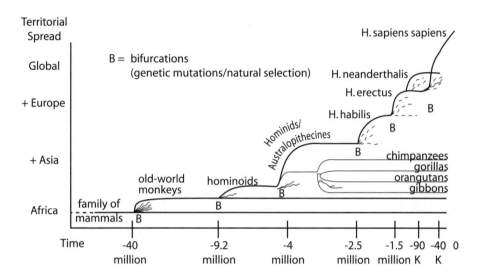

The progressive if strongly nonlinear evolution of biological systems gave rise to a plethora of biological species, and led to the extinction of a majority of them. It also gave birth to the lineage of hominids. The family of primates split off from the then existing species of mammals around 40 million years ago. The first primates were the old-world monkeys that populated wide areas of Asia and Africa. Then, about 9.2 million years ago, the primate family split into two groups. One, the pongids, stayed with the arboreal life and, whereas several branches (such as *Gigantopithecus* and *Sivapithecus*) subsequently became extinct, the survivors evolved into the modern apes: chimpanzees, gorillas, orangutans, and gibbons. The other group became terrestrially based bipedalists: the family of hominids.

About four million years ago, the early hominid *Australopithecines* were widely distributed in eastern and southern Africa. Living in small bands, they managed to survive the dangers of terrestrial life. About 2.5 million years ago, they split into different branches. A branch that became extinct included numerous subspecies, such as *boisei* and *robustus,* while the surviving branch led to *habilis* and *erectus,* and ultimately to *sapiens.*

Although the details of hominid evolution are not definitively established, it appears that modern man, *Homo sapiens sapiens,* evolved from hominid ancestors in Africa. Some 40,000 years ago, sapiens appeared in Europe, probably co-inhabiting the continent with *Homo neanderthalis.* The latter disappeared around 30,000 years ago, making *Homo sapiens sapiens* the sole survivor of the hominid branch.

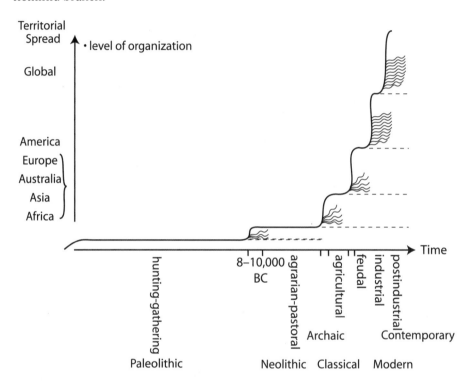

With *Homo sapiens sapiens,* evolution shifted from the biological to the sociocultural dimension. For the past 30,000 years or so, the alternating periods of stability and instability no longer involved the genetic code of humans, but involved their society and culture. Since that time, it has been the sociocultural organization of groups of individuals that has mutated: how people related to each other and to their environment, what values and ethics they adopted, and how they saw themselves and the world around them.

In the course of the past 10,000 years, a series of sociocultural mutations produced a vast range of organizational forms, from Paleolithic Stone-Age tribes and Neolithic agrarian communities, through the archaic empires of Babylonia, Egypt, India, and China, to the European feudal kingdoms and princedoms. More than

300 years ago, the system of modern nation-states appeared: Industrial societies were born. We are now at the threshold of a sociocultural mutation beyond the nation-state system, to a more integrated postindustrial civilization.

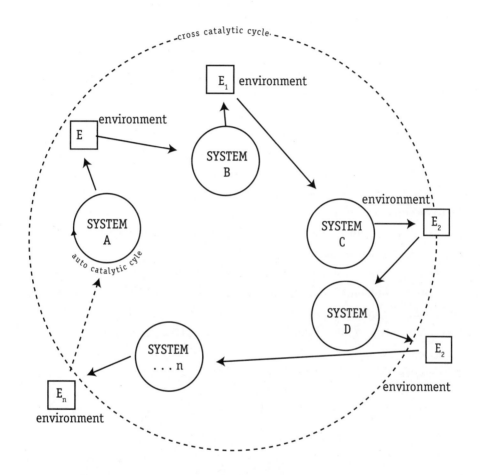

Each emerging form of sociocultural organization embraces, integrates, and partially transforms the previous forms. It creates a new, higher-level system, of which the previous systems become functional subsystems.

The formation of higher-level "suprasystems" through the interlinking of previously relatively autonomous systems (which are thereafter subsystems) is a familiar notion in systems theory. Suprasystems emerge through the creation of "hypercycles" in which the subsystems are linked by cycles that mutually catalyze each other: so-called cross-catalytic cycles. The result is that the subsystems become increasingly interdependent, while the suprasystem jointly constituted by them takes on structure and autonomy.

Nobel laureate physicist Manfred Eigen has shown that suprasystem-formation through auto- and cross-catalytic cycles is the basis of the evolution of all life on the planet. In the rich molecular soup of the primeval seas, cross-catalytic cycles were naturally selected over other kinds of linkages; they had more stability in a turbulent environment than any other form of molecular organization. Thermodynamicist and physical chemist Ilya Prigogine was awarded the Nobel Prize for working out the way cross-catalytic cycles lead to the evolution of complex systems.

Cross-catalytic cycles also operate in human society. In the political sphere, intensifying ties among nation-states have produced progressive shifts from the national to the regional, and then to the global level of organization. Regional economic groupings such as the European Union and the Association of Southeast Asian Nations were formed, and they linked up with global international and intergovernmental organizations. Together they now assume a number of the functions previously vested in national governments.

An analogous process unfolds in the business world. By means of mergers and acquisitions, outsourcing, and various forms of cooperation and partnerships, enterprises first created on the local level branch out on the national level, and then move to the multinational and even to the global level. The brand name of the global players identifies the hypercycle that integrates the company's various subsidiaries, subdivisions, and business units.

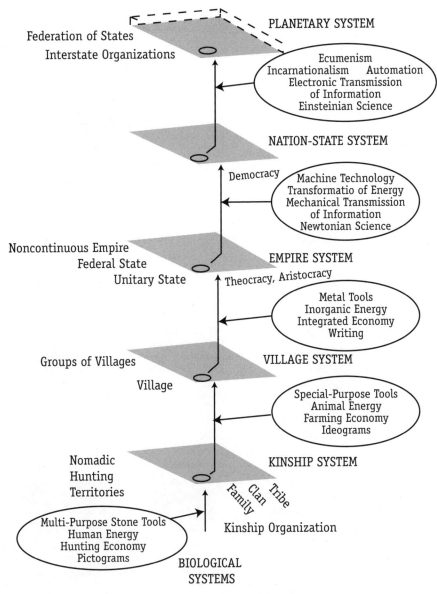

Federation of States
Interstate Organizations

PLANETARY SYSTEM

Ecumenism
Incarnationalism   Automation
Electronic Transmission
of Information
Einsteinian Science

NATION-STATE SYSTEM

Democracy

Machine Technology
Transformatio of Energy
Mechanical Transmission
of Information
Newtonian Science

Noncontinuous Empire
Federal State
Unitary State

EMPIRE SYSTEM

Theocracy, Aristocracy

Metal Tools
Inorganic Energy
Integrated Economy
Writing

Groups of Villages

VILLAGE SYSTEM

Village

Special-Purpose Tools
Animal Energy
Farming Economy
Ideograms

Nomadic
Hunting
Territories

KINSHIP SYSTEM

Tribe
Clan
Family

Multi-Purpose Stone Tools
Human Energy
Hunting Economy
Pictograms

Kinship Organization

BIOLOGICAL
SYSTEMS

(Contributed by Alastair M. Taylor)

The nonlinear but on the whole progressive evolution of societies is driven by innovations that perturb and eventually destabilize previously stable systems. The innovations are *technological* innovations in the sense of technology as any hardware or software by means of which people relate to each other and to their environment.

99

Industrial Revolution

Motive Power
x 10^3 increase

1 horsepower   1,000 horsepower

Information Revolution

1970   2000

Computing Power
performance = 10^5 increase
cost = 10^3 decrease

10^3 transistors/chip 10^8 transistors/chip

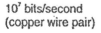

Communications Power
performance = 10^4 increase
cost = 10^2 decrease

10^7 bits/second 10^{11} bits/second
(copper wire pair)   (optical fiber)

Technological innovations began when our forebears developed a symbolic language, conceptual thinking, and cooperative tool use. In the course of history, the accelerating series of such innovations involved ever more people and ever more extensive territories. It now propels societies toward the global level.

The next sociocultural mutation will be driven by a new technological innovation: the "information revolution." The technologies of information and communication that are presently destabilizing the established structures of industrial societies have a far more global reach, and the "revolutions" they create unfold several dimensions faster than the steam and fossil-fuel-based technologies of the first Industrial Revolution.

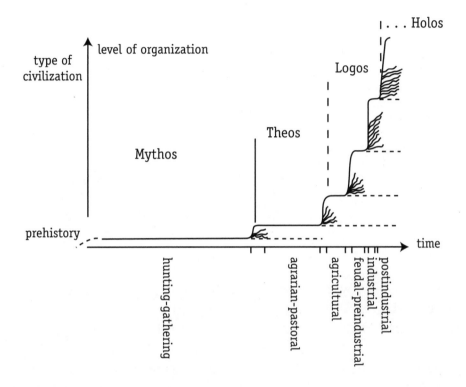

Driven by the staggering pace of innovation in the information/communication sector, humanity finds itself at the threshold of a sociocultural mutation beyond classical industrial civilization. If the systems do not break down, the next mutation will see the birth of a planetary civilization capable of coping with the "fluctuations" that rock the societies, economies, and enterprises of the industrialized era—the civilization of Holos.

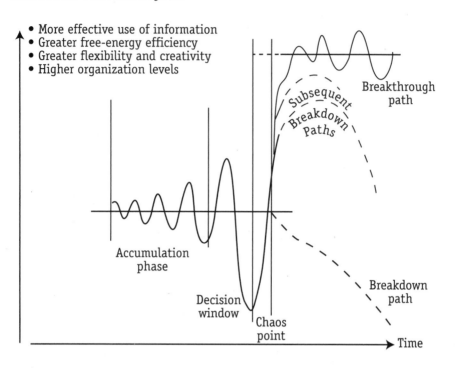

- More effective use of information
- Greater free-energy efficiency
- Greater flexibility and creativity
- Higher organization levels

Breakthrough path

Subsequent Breakdown Paths

Accumulation phase

Decision window

Chaos point

Breakdown path

Time

We live in a window in time between industrial-age Logos civilization and a yet-to-be-achieved civilization of Holos. Achieving the latter is not assured: The current window allows alternative outcomes. But before long, we shall reach a global tipping point—the Chaos Point—and then our world will evolve either one way or another. This point will be reached when critical processes—conflicts and stresses in society, inequality in the distribution of resources in the economy, and the degeneration of vital balances in the ecology—reach a phase of irreversibility. Our systems will be launched on a trajectory either toward breakdown or toward breakthrough. Which trajectory will be selected is not determined in advance; the current decision-window has a high degree of indeterminacy, and hence of autonomy.

The indeterminacy and autonomy of mutations in biological systems make the precise outcome unpredictable. In a human system, on the other hand, while the indeterminacy and autonomy of cultural mutation is real, the unpredictability of the outcome is mitigated. This is due to the presence of consciousness. Conscious members of the social system can grasp the nature of the evolutionary processes that unfold around them and can purposefully intervene. At a decision-window, individuals can consciously create the small but potentially powerful fluctuations that could "blow up" and decide the evolutionary path their society will adopt.

They can tip the system toward the evolution that is in line with their hopes and expectations. Thus the Chaos Point need not be the harbinger of global breakdown. It could be the herald of a leap to a new civilization.

The foregoing ten graphics illustrated where we are and how we got here. They cannot illustrate where we will go from here, only where we *could* go. Where we *will* go is still up to us.

Appendix A

How I Came to Be Involved with Global Questions and the Club of Budapest—An Autobiographical Note

A whole series of events, in themselves unremarkable, pushed and pulled me toward involvement with questions and problems of the world community and its future. The series began with a phone call from Professor Richard Falk of Princeton University's Center of International Studies. This was in the early 1970s. I was teaching at the time in the philosophy department of the State University of New York at Geneseo, in the quiet rural regions of upstate New York, immersed in the attempt to elucidate the implications of thinking in terms of integral systems rather than isolated entities. I had just started to develop the evolutionary dimensions of general system theory, moving toward what I subsequently called "general evolution theory" (that is, a general theory of evolution as it applies to physical systems, living systems, consciousness, and even to the universe as a system).

The call from Dick Falk was unexpected. Although I had known that he did valuable work in the framework of the World Order Models Project, I knew nothing about what world models were, how successful they were, and what problems they encountered. Yet Dick asked me to come to Princeton to give a series of seminars on the "world system." I explained my ignorance of the subject to him, but Dick was not to be deterred: He said that it would be sufficient that I present my conception of complex evolving systems: He and other members of the Center's faculty would see how they could be applied to the world system. I was dubious, but the challenge was intriguing, and I accepted.

This was the first and, as it turned out, decisive step toward my involvement with the world system and its problems and prospects. Out of my seminars at Princeton came a book, *A Strategy for the Future: The Systems Approach to World Order* (1974). It reached the hands of Aurelio Peccei, the visionary founder and then-president of the Club of Rome. Aurelio was just then wondering how to elaborate the more immediately human implications of the Club's first report, the legendary *Limits to Growth*. He asked for my advice and, following our initial exchange, asked that I set up a project to look at what aspirations people and societies have in regard to the future—and to what extent these aspirations can be fulfilled on a finite planet.

Within six months I assembled a small but enthusiastic team of young scholars and budding activists. We developed the "Goals for Mankind" project, and presented it to Aurelio. He and Alex King, the cofounder of the Club of Rome, liked it, and my team set about implementing it. As this required vast international contacts (there was no e-mail and Internet at the time), Aurelio asked Davidson Nicol, the executive director of the UN "think tank," UNITAR (United Nations Institute for Training and Research), to invite me to work at the Institute where worldwide communication facilities were available. I was named Special Fellow and moved to New York City, bringing the core team with me.

We settled down to work. Our *Report to the Club of Rome* was completed in about a year and was published first in English and then in various other languages (*Goals for Mankind: The New Horizons of Global Community*, 1978). My task accomplished, I returned to the quiet upstate campus of the State University of New York in the comforting belief that I could pick up my work in systems theory, having concluded my involvement with humanity's future.

But another phone call came a few weeks later, this time from Davidson Nicol: He asked me to represent the Institute at the founding of the United Nations University in Tokyo. I could not refuse, and one thing led to another. First Nicol asked me to head the Institute's research on the New International Economic Order, an ambitious world project that was to be adopted by the UN General Assembly at a special session devoted to it in the fall of 1980. Working at the Institute at its UN headquarters, I had the opportunity to create an international network of more than 90 research institutes. By 1980, we had published eleven volumes of studies in the "NIEO Library," a series of books created for us by Pergamon Press in Oxford.

The NIEO project came to an abrupt end when at the Special Session three major economic powers—the U.S., the UK, and West Germany—announced that they "do not participate" in voting for the proposed resolution. The NIEO as an economic objective and UN-backed political project was forthwith abandoned.

Then Kurt Waldheim, the secretary general at the time, asked what ideas I might have to relaunch the dialogue between North and South. I suggested a systemic concept. Let's not attempt to move from the level of the nation-state directly to the global level of North and South, I said, but first prepare the ground by helping the South to become a better balanced and less dependent partner in negotiations with the industrialized countries. This would call for effective economic and social integration organizations bringing together groups of developing countries, following the example (but not necessarily the model) of the European Community.

The project "Regional and Interregional Cooperation among Developing Countries" was adopted by UNITAR at the end of 1980. I managed to bring together a high-level "Panel of Eminent Persons" to present the conclusions to the secretary general—who in turn was to present them to the General Assembly. This project took another four years of intensive effort. We produced four volumes of background studies and the draft of a Declaration on what we called RCDC: Regional Cooperation Among Developing Countries. The Declaration was signed and ready to be presented to the secretary general, who at the time was Javier Pérez de Cuéllar.

Mr. Pérez de Cuéllar told me that he had read the document and would be willing to present it, but he "cannot recognize it." It turned out that the secretary general can only "recognize" documents prepared by the Secretariat when they are presented by the appropriate member of his cabinet. The undersecretary responsible for research had changed just beforehand (the term of the previous undersecretary having expired), and the new man did not submit the document on the principle that if he did not initiate and implement a project, it did not merit to be furthered. The RCDC project ended right there. The effort was not entirely wasted, however, because in the years that followed, a number of regional organizations studied our recommendations and implemented them to the extent they found economically feasible and politically expedient.

After seven years of coping with challenges, responsibilities, and intrigues at the United Nations, I could not face returning to the ivory-tower seclusion of my university; I retired instead to the bucolic seclusion of the 300-year-old farm-house in Tuscany I had had the good fortune to acquire ten years before. I intended to take a sabbatical year, to catch up with developments in the field of general system and general evolution theory. That year never ended, however, since first Professor Kinhide Mushakoji (then vice chancellor of the UN University) and then Federico Mayor (the newly elected director general of UNESCO) called on me to serve as advisor, and later as collaborator. As a result, in addition to reading and writing in my chosen field of interest, I spent consid-erable time working for the European Perspectives Program of the UNU, and developing and carrying out a project exploring the potentials of unity within the world's cultural diversity for UNESCO.

I had not forgotten a promise I made to Aurelio Peccei in 1978, on the occa-sion of the ten-year anniversary meeting of the Club of Rome in the city of Rome. This was to create a sister club made up of artists, writers, and spiritual leaders. The rationale was the recognition that addressing leaders in politics and business is not sufficient to move beyond lip service to new ideas and strategies—we must also mobilize the thinking, the imagination, and the creativity of people in main-stream society. For this, we knew, we had to call on individuals whose words and personality engage the public's attention and respect.

I spoke on the need for an "artists and writers' club" from time to time, but failed to make headway: People thought it was a good idea but nobody offered to provide the seed money to implement it. This changed when I presented the con-cept at the Third World Congress of Hungarians in Budapest. Jozsef Antal, then Prime Minister of Hungary, was present at the event and he called me the next day, wanting to hear more. When he did, he spontaneously offered to set up a secre-tariat for such a club in Budapest. I accepted gratefully, and we agreed that, follow-ing the example of the Club of Rome (which was named after the city where the original meeting took place), we should call it "Club of Budapest."

The idea of this club proved attractive, and a number of famous personalities agreed to join, beginning with the president of Hungary, Arpad Goncz (himself a writer), and soon followed by the Dalai Lama, Yehudi Menuhin, and Peter Ustinov. By the end of the first year we had Vaclav Havel, Mikhail Gorbachev, Liv Ullmann, Peter Gabriel, and three dozen similar names on our roster of "Hono-rary Members."

Working in consultation with a board of advisors, I decided to focus on the evolution of human consciousness as the key issue the club was to address. This was prompted by my recollection that, when discussing the results of international conferences and conventions, those who drew up the agenda would say that although the objectives might be applauded, they would not really be implemented. When queried why, they would say the political will was lacking. And when asked why it was lacking, some would say that the leader's and their constituency's consciousness was not sufficiently evolved to perceive the need. I suggested that we should begin where others had ended: with the issue of raising people's consciousness. Together with our friends and advisors I drafted a Manifesto on the need for a new consciousness and showed it to the Dalai Lama. Without further ado, he canceled his next appointments and set about elaborating it. Three hours later we had the basic text of what members of the Club of Budapest had further specified and then adopted: the "Manifesto on the Spirit of Planetary Consciousness" (reproduced in appendix C).

After this, there was no turning back. For the past twelve years I have been dividing my time and energy between Tuscany and Budapest, researching the meaning of the ever-more-fabulous findings coming to light at the frontiers of the new sciences, and working for the Club of Budapest in creating and implementing projects under the motto "you can change the world."

On the 9th of September, 2009, the auspicious date 09.09.09, we had launched the WorldShift 2012 movement at the British Museum in London. This initiative brought together likeminded organizations and forward-looking individuals from all parts of the world. They came to form the critical mass that could catalyze the larger critical mass that would be powerful enough to shift the world.

Appendix B

Comments by Members and Partners of the Club of Budapest

The Members Comment

Peter Russell . . . on the roots of the global crisis

As Ervin Laszlo makes clear, the global crisis we are now facing is, at its root, a crisis of culture and consciousness. Certainly, we need to do everything in our power to curb population growth and reduce the impact our technology has on the planet's ecosystems. But we also need to ask why it is that one species out of millions—a species that considers itself the most intelligent species on this planet—can behave in ways that are clearly not in its long-term self-interest. To realize that we are threatening our own survival, and that of many other species, and then to continue with the very activities that are causing the problem, is nothing short of insane.

The root of the problem lies in our thinking, our attitudes, and our values. We are stuck in an outdated mindset that tells us that if we are to be at peace, we need to have the right things. Such an attitude may be important when individual survival is at stake; we need then to focus our attention on our physical well-being. But this is not an issue for most people in the developed world. The world has changed beyond all recognition from preindustrial times, and most of our survival needs are now met. But because we have not changed our thinking, we continue to consume and despoil the planet in the vain hope that if only we had enough of the right things, we would find fulfillment. Today it is our collective survival that is at stake, and it is our inner, spiritual well-being that most urgently needs our care and attention.

This is the challenge of the early twenty-first century: exploration of inner space—the development of human consciousness to match the fantastic strides we have made in our material development.

Edgar Mitchell . . . on the challenge, and the vision of science

As one of those who has had the privilege of observing this magnificent little planet from the darkness of space, I join my colleagues of the Club of Budapest who call for a new vision for the future and a new dedication to the proper stewardship of our planet.

From above the protective canopy of our atmosphere, one can observe the progressive degradation of the ecological systems on which all species depend for sustenance. It is clear from that view and with data from four decades of space activity that our burgeoning population has set a course that is not sustainable. We are a species that is incessantly in conflict over mundane issues while ignoring the chasm that lies ahead for us all. We argue from the point of view of our traditional cultural values, unwilling to look at ourselves from the larger global perspective and to take the necessary steps to create a more tranquil and harmonious civilization for our mutual benefit—steps that include some hard choices about our lifestyles.

In the past two decades, scientists have advanced a significant number of concepts that, when taken together and applied to the metaproblem envisaged through general evolution and systems theory, provide a radically new understanding of the human condition and our place in the cosmos. I refer to experiments in quantum physics that demonstrate "nonlocality" (meaning interconnectedness) at the level of subatomic particles; "quantum holography," which extends that idea to macroscale objects; and work in chaos theory, which suggests the repetition of basic structures across scale sizes from the microscopic to the cosmic. In addition, chaos theory and the theory of complex systems suggest the presence of simple feedback loops that organize the basic structures and processes of nature into the exquisite shapes we find in living matter. I refer to the work of the astronomers and cosmologists who continue to discover the marvels of distant worlds and to the work of Ilya Prigogine, who has shown that the most fundamental processes in nature are the nonlinear processes, not the simple, linear, reversible processes that scientists have studied since Newton's time.

The effect of all this is the view that we live in a self-organizing, creative, intelligent, learning, trial-and-error universe that has evolved to "know" itself and has likely spawned intelligent life throughout its expanse. Virtually all the numinous events reported by the esoteric core in every cultural tradition—events that serve as the basis for traditional religious lore—can now be understood in terms that should satisfy the most critical scientist. The lessons from this view for our times pertain to our evolution as creative, interconnected, and responsible humans with the fate of our world and all its species resting in our collective hands, dependent on our vision and wisdom to chart a sustainable course into the future.

We have the knowledge, the wisdom, and the visionaries among us to enable us to understand today's critical issues. We must now find the collective political will to implement and accelerate the necessary steps on a global basis—or suffer the consequences.

Karan Singh . . . on the evolution of the new consciousness

We live in a shrinking world in which the heritage of conflict and competition, and the growing gap between the developed and the developing world, will have to make way for a new culture of convergence and cooperation if the rich promise of the new millennium is not to dissolve into conflict and chaos.

Unprecedented human interventions in the environment have upset the delicate ecological balance that enabled Mother Earth—Bhavani Vasundhara in the Indian tradition, Gaia in the Greek—to survive for billions of years and become a unique crucible for the evolution of consciousness. Ruthless exploitation of nonrenewable natural resources has created havoc and, if allowed to continue, may result in a series of major ecological disasters that will disrupt life on this planet in the twenty-first century.

We do not lack the intellectual or economic resources to tackle the problems. Scientific breakthroughs and technological ingenuity have given us the capacity to overcome all challenges. What is missing is the wisdom and compassion to do so. Knowledge proliferates, but wisdom languishes. This yawning chasm needs to be bridged before the end of this decade if we are ever to reverse the present trend toward disaster.

The astounding communications system encircling the globe today seldom uses its tremendous potential to spread global values and foster a more caring, compassionate consciousness. On the contrary, the media is full of violence and horror, cruelty and carnage, unbridled consumerism and unabashed promiscuity, which not only distorts the awareness of the young but dulls our sensitivity to the problems of human suffering and pain. What is urgently needed, therefore, is a U-turn in our educational and communications policies. We need to develop carefully structured programs on a global scale based clearly and unequivocally on the premise that human survival involves the growth of a creative and compassionate planetary consciousness. The spiritual dimension must once again be given importance in our thinking, and for this we must draw upon the great reservoir of idealism and spiritual values provided by the rich religious traditions of humanity.

We need the courage to think globally, to break away from traditional paradigms, and to plunge boldly into the future. We must so mobilize our inner and outer resources that we can in the twenty-first century consciously build a new world based on mutually assured welfare rather than mutually assured destruction.

As global citizens committed to human survival and welfare, we must structure a worldwide program of education—for children and adults alike—that will open their eyes to the reality of the dawning global age and their hearts to the cries of the oppressed and the suffering. There is no time to be lost, because, along with the emergence of global society, the sinister forces of fundamentalism and fanaticism, of exploitation and intimidation, are active as well.

Let us, then, with utmost speed, pioneer and propagate a new, holistic consciousness based on the following premises:

1. That the planet we inhabit and of which we are all citizens—Planet Earth—is a single, living, pulsating entity; that the human race in the final analysis is an interlocking, extended family—Vasudhaiva Kutumbakam, as the Veda has it; and that differences of race and religion, nationality and ideology, sex and sexual preference, economic and social status, though significant in themselves, must be viewed in the broader context of global unity.

2. That the ecology of Planet Earth has to be preserved from mindless destruction and ruthless exploitation and enriched for the welfare of generations yet unborn; and that there must be a more equitable consumption pattern based on limits to growth, not unbridled consumerism.

3. That hatred and bigotry, fundamentalism and fanaticism, greed and jealousy, whether among individuals, groups, or nations, are corrosive emotions that must be overcome as we move into the next century; and that love and compassion, caring and charity, friendship and cooperation are the elements that have to be encouraged as we transit into our new global awareness.

4. That the world's great religions must no longer war against each other for supremacy, but mutually cooperate for the welfare of the human race, and that, instead of feeding the dogma and exclusivism that divide them, a continuing and creative interfaith dialogue must nurture the golden thread of spiritual aspiration that binds them together.

5. That a new, holistic education must acknowledge the multiple dimensions of the human personality—physical, intellectual, aesthetic, emotional, and spiritual—and seek a harmonious development of the integrated human being.

Ever since I first saw it two decades ago, I have been fascinated by the amazing photograph taken from the moon showing our planet as it really is: a tiny speck of light and life, so beautiful and yet so fragile, ablaze with the fire of consciousness against the blackness of outer space. This Earth, looked upon in so many cultures as the Mother, has nurtured the evolution of consciousness from the slime of the primeval ocean billions of years ago to where we stand today. Now, in a dramatic reversal, it is we who must nurture this Earth, to repair the scars that in our hubris we have inflicted on her and safeguard the welfare of all creatures that inhabit her today and in millennia to come. This further evolution of our consciousness must surely be the guiding vision for all of us in the attempt to structure a humane society in the twenty-first century.

Thomas Berry . . . on the historical mission of our times

I summarize my own thinking in a single sentence with seven phrases: The historical mission of our times is to reinvent the human at the species level, with critical reflection, within the community of life systems, in a time-developmental context, by means of story and shared dream experience.

First, I say "reinvent the human" because the issues we are concerned with seem beyond the competence of our present cultural traditions. As humans, more than any other mode of being, we give shape and form to ourselves in our cultural configurations. We are genetically coded toward a further transgenetic coding whereby we articulate the human mode of being. We are genetically coded to think. We do not have a choice to think or not to think. We do have a choice of what we think and how we shape our patterns of living, our moral codes, our social institutions, and our artistic and literary traditions. What is needed is something beyond our existing traditions to bring us back to the most fundamental aspect of the human. The issue has never been as critical as it is now. The human is at an impasse. We have been using our freedom of determination to set ourselves at odds with the entire nonhuman community of earthly existence. We need to give a cultural form to ourselves that is coherent with the larger community of existence.

Second, we must work "at the species level" because our problems are beyond any existing cultural solution. We must return to our genetic coding. Our problems are at the species and interspecies level. This is clear in every aspect of the human. As regards economics, we need not simply a national or a global economy but a species and interspecies economy. Presently, our schools of business teach the skills whereby the greatest possible number of natural resources is processed as quickly as possible, put through the consumer economy, and then passed on to the junk heap where it is useless at best and toxic to every living being at worst. There is need for the human species to develop reciprocal economic relationships with other life forms, providing a sustaining pattern of mutual support, as is the case with other life systems.

As regards law, we need a species legal tradition that would provide for the legal rights of geological and biological as well as human components of the Earth community. A legal system exclusively for humans is not realistic. Habitat, for example, must be given legal status as sacred and inviolable for every mode of being.

Third, I say "with critical reflection" because this reinventing of the human needs to be done with critical competence. We need all our scientific knowledge. We cannot abandon our technologies. We must, however, see that our technologies cohere to the technologies of the natural world. Our knowledge needs to be a creative response to the natural world rather than a domination of the natural world.

Fourth, we need to reinvent the human "within the community of life systems." Because the Earth is not adequately understood either by our spiritual or by our scientific traditions, the human has become an addendum or an intrusion. We have found this situation to our liking because it enables us to avoid the problem of presence integral to the Earth. This attitude prevents us from considering the Earth as a single society with ethical relations determined primarily by the well-being of the total Earth community.

But while the Earth is a single integral community, it is not a global sameness. It is highly differentiated in bioregional communities—in arctic as well as tropical regions, in mountains, valleys, plains, and coastal regions. These bioregions can be described as identifiable geographical areas of interacting life systems that are relatively self-sustaining in the ever-renewing processes of nature. As the functional units of the planet, these bioregions can be described as self-propagating, self-nourishing, self-educating, self-governing, self-healing, and self-fulfilling communities.

Fifth, reinventing the human must take place in "a time-developmental context." We now understand the universe and the planet Earth not simply as an ever-renewing sequence of seasonal transformations; it is also an emergent process going through an irreversible sequence of transformation episodes, moving in general from lesser to greater complexity in structure, from lesser to greater modes of consciousness, from lesser to greater freedoms. This constitutes what might be called the cosmological dimension of the program of the Club of Budapest. Our sense of who we are and what our role is must begin where the universe begins. Not only our physical shaping, but also our spiritual and cultural shaping begins with the formation of the universe.

Sixth, from the previous, we can appreciate the directing and energizing role played by "the story of the universe." This story that we know through empirical observation is our most valuable resource in establishing a viable mode of being for the human species as well as for all those stupendous life systems whereby the Earth achieves its grandeur, its fertility, and its capacity for continuing self-renewal. This story—as told in its galactic expansion, its Earth formation, its life emergence, and its consciousness manifestation in the human—fulfills in our times the role of the mythic accounts of the universe that existed in earlier times when human awareness was dominated by a spatial mode of consciousness. We have moved from cosmos to cosmogenesis, from the mandala journey to the center of an abiding world, to the great irreversible journey of the universe itself as the primary sacred journey.

This journey of the universe is the journey of each individual being in the universe. The great journey is an exciting revelatory story that gives us our macrophase identity—the larger dimensions of meaning that we need. To be able to identify the microphase of our being with the macrophase mode of our being is the quintessence of what needs to be achieved.

The present imperative of the human is that this journey continue on into the future in the integrity of the unfolding life systems of the Earth, which presently are threatened in their survival. Our great failure is the termination of the journey for so many of the most brilliant species of the life community. The horrendous fact is that we are, as Norman Myers has indicated, in an extinction spasm that is likely to produce "the greatest single setback of life's abundance and diversity since the first flickerings of life almost four billion years ago." The labor and care expended over some billion years and untold billions of experiments to bring forth such a gorgeous Earth may be negated by something mistakenly considered progress toward a better life in a better world.

The seventh and final aspect of my statement concerning the ethical imperative of our times is the "shared dream experience." The creative process, whether in the human or the cosmological order, is too mysterious for easy explanation. Yet we all have experience of creative activity. Human processes involve much trial and error, with only occasional success at any high level of distinction, and we may well believe that the cosmological process has also passed through a vast period of experimentation in order to achieve the ordered processes of our present universe.

In both instances, something is perceived in a dim and uncertain manner, something radiant with meaning that draws us on to a further clarification of our understanding and our activity. Suddenly, out of the formless condition, a formed reality appears. This process can be described in many ways, as a groping or as a feeling or as an imaginative process. The most appropriate way of describing this process seems to be that of dream realization. The universe appears to be the fulfillment of something so highly imaginative and so overwhelming that it must have been dreamed into existence.

But if the dream is creative, we must also recognize that few things are so destructive as a dream or entrancement that has lost the integrity of its meaning and become an exaggerated and destructive manifestation. This has happened often enough with political ideologies and with religious visionaries, but there is no dream or entrancement in the history of the Earth that has wrought the destruction taking place in the entrancement with industrial civilization. Such entrancement must be considered as a profound cultural pathology. It can be dealt with only by a correspondingly deep cultural therapy. This healing therapy can be successful only if associated with a creative vision capable of giving birth to a new, more integral expression of the entire planetary process.

Such is our present situation. We are involved not simply with an ethical issue but with a disturbance sanctioned by the very structures of the culture itself in its present phase. The destructive dream of the twentieth century appears as a kind of ultimate manifestation of that deep inner rage of Western society against its earthly condition as a vital member of the life community. As with the goose that laid the golden egg, so the Earth is assaulted in a vain effort to possess not simply the magnificent fruits of the Earth but the power itself whereby these splendors have emerged.

At such a moment, a new revelatory experience is needed, an experience wherein human consciousness awakens to the grandeur and sacred quality of the Earth process. This awakening is our human participation in the dream of the Earth, the dream that is carried in its integrity, not in any one of Earth's cultural expressions but in the depths of our genetic coding. Therein the Earth functions at a depth beyond our capacity for conscious awareness. We can only be sensitized to what is revealed to us. Such participation in the dream of the Earth we probably have not had since our earlier shamanic times, but therein lies our hope for the future for ourselves and the entire Earth community.

Robert Muller . . . on consciousness and the global emergency

In 50 years of world service with the United Nations, I have come to consider the birth of planetary consciousness, together with the creation of global institutions and the convening of world conferences, the major hopes for enabling humanity to cope with the acute problems facing us. In view of the current resistance, slowness, if not opposition of many governments to act on the various intergovernmental agreements on the environment, and being a member of the Club of Budapest, I consider it my duty to make the following recommendations:

1. To declare a state of emergency of the Earth.

2. To consider the present situation as an outright war: a World War III against nature and its elements, a war that must now end.

3. To request a second world conference on the biosphere, 30 years after the first one in 1978, to ascertain the state of the biosphere today.

4. To support the extension to other countries of the World Party of Natural Law already existing in 85 countries at the initiative of British scientists.

5. To place our weight behind a radical change in the political system of our planet, a system that currently provides services and financial resources to local

communities, cities, provinces, and nations, but leaves the Earth and the human family almost entirely without adequate services and financial resources at a time when these are most urgently needed.

6. In view of the chaos of the nation-state system and its colossal duplication of services and their financial costs (e.g., the national military establishments), to urgently agree on the absolute and imperative necessity to create, whether sooner or later but unavoidably, a proper Earth Government in the form of a Federal Government, of a United States of the World, or of a Union based on the model of the European Union of five continental Unions with a global superstructure, or of a government patterned on bioregional or bio-organizational models suggested by nature herself.

In the absence of such initiatives, we are likely to see the disappearance of most life forms, including human life, from this planet in the course of the twenty-first century.

Riane Eisler . . . on partnership and the new consciousness

The human community faces an epochal challenge: how to bring about the changes in consciousness required if we are to have a more equitable and sustainable future. Human consciousness does not spring up in a vacuum: It is shaped by culture. That is why at this evolutionary crossroads—when we and our natural habitat are being, as never before, reshaped by technology—cultural evolution is as important as biological evolution, and in some ways more so.

Over the last 300 years we have seen great changes in consciousness: challenges to beliefs and institutions that were not so long ago viewed as "just the way things are." These challenges were initiated by small, unpopular, and often persecuted minorities conscious that we humans have alternatives—that man's domination of nature, of women, and of "lesser" men is neither divinely ordained nor biologically prefigured.

As this consciousness spread, mass movements sprang up, challenging the supposedly divinely ordained right of kings to rule their "subjects," of men to rule women and children in the "castles" of their homes, of "superior" races to rule "inferior" ones, of warlike tribes and nations to conquer more peaceful ones, and, most recently, of our species to overpopulate, despoil, and pollute the planetary habitat.

Although we do not yet think of them in these terms, these movements are not random and disconnected, and neither is resistance to them. Underneath the currents and countercurrents of history lies the dynamic tension between two basic possibilities of human culture: partnership and domination. Each of these models has a very different configuration that is visible once we become conscious of a generally ignored interactive systems dynamic: that relations in the private and the public spheres are inextricably intertwined. In fact, it is through our intimate relations that we first learn, and then continually practice respect for, or violation of, human rights as well as respect for, or disregard of, the natural habitat. Through these relations that involve touch to the body, our intimate sexual relations as well as our early childhood relations, we internalize, on a deeply unconscious neurological level, how two bodies should relate. If we are to effectively change consciousness in the direction needed for human and planetary survival, it is necessary to address the critical matter of how consciousness is culturally formed and replicated.

One of the great challenges we face is how to awaken contemporary consciousness to the possibility—and urgent necessity—of relations based primarily on partnership rather than domination, in both the private and the public sphere. In this regard, we must dispel some prevailing myths about what is popularly called "human nature"—our biological constraints and possibilities. Despite myths that we humans are base, flawed by either original sin or selfish genes, the most profound human yearning rooted in our biological evolution is for caring connection. Indeed, despite our conditioning for thousands of years for dominator rather than partnership relations with one another and with nature, we have an inherent capacity, indeed an inherent drive, toward relations based on partnership. Despite beliefs and institutions that have rewarded, and even idealized, cruelty and violence (as in our "heroic" epics), we have an enormous capacity for caring and for altruistic behaviors—as demonstrated, for example, by the women and men who during the Nazi era risked their lives and those of their families to save Jews. Notwithstanding myths that men naturally want to dominate women and women naturally want to be dominated, women and men worldwide have been moving toward relations based on partnership in both the public and the private sphere. Despite adages such as "spare the rod and spoil the child" and the notion that violence can be the instrument of our deliverance (still propagated by some fundamentalist religious authorities), the institution of war, as well as such institutionalized forms of intimate violence as wife and child beating, have been increasingly challenged. And, as this book shows, despite the continuing idealization of "man's conquest of nature," the consciousness of our interconnections with all forms of life on this planet is beginning to reemerge.

For the past three centuries, we have seen a major revolution in consciousness: the emergence in bits and pieces of the consciousness that a partnership way of structuring human society and culture is a viable possibility. We have also begun to see the recognition of something else: that we humans are the only species we know of who have consciously attempted to create a more equitable and sustainable society—once again suggesting that not only is a partnership form of social organization essential at this point in our cultural and technological evolution, but it is also the form we need if we are to develop our uniquely human potentials.

It is this emerging Holos consciousness—and the active efforts of each one of us to spread it through all our institutions, from the family and religion to politics, economics, education, and the mass media—that offers us realistic hope for our future and that of generations still to come.

Edgar Morin . . . on the evolutionary path

A globalized situation calls for a global response. Such a response will have to be prepared, initiated, and stimulated by local initiatives. We are in a dialectical movement of parts and wholes: the parts contribute to the whole. In this sense, national states can play a decisive role—provided that, in their own interest, they abandon pretensions of absolute sovereignty with regard to the great issues of common interest, issues of life and death. These go far beyond their own national competence. The productive era of nation-states wielding absolute power is past. This does not mean that nation-states have to be disintegrated, rather, that they need to be integrated in greater wholes with regard to the vital imperatives of the planet of which they themselves are a part.

The issue is all the more crucial because, as an indirect consequence, the process of globalization gives rise to balkanization and national and ethnocentric recalcitrance. An evolutionary path can open up only in the dialectic of the local and the global, the national and the worldwide, out of the conjunction and synergy of various forces and tendencies progressing in a salutary direction. This path must allow:

1. The universal spread of the social providence of the state (which entails the de-bureaucratization of heavy state machinery).

2. The regulation or slowing of international economic competition. This presupposes the action of international, "trinitarian" (economic, ecologic, cultural) authorities equally as competent to fight against ecological degradation as

a result of uncontrolled growth as against cultural degradation due to sweeping westernization.

3. The design of a civilization-enhancing policy to halt the processes of destruction and self-destruction generated by the globalization of Western society. This policy needs to regenerate and foster the humanist, rational, civil, critical, and self-critical virtues that have also been created in this process, virtues that are necessary ingredients in the reform of civilization.

4. The emergence of a planetary citizenship with branches all over the world through humanitarian and ecologic associations and nongovernmental organizations concerned with development, the rights of women, the protection of minorities, and the like.

5. The strengthening of the consciousness of people that they belong to the Earth as our shared homeland. This Holos consciousness implies not only a keen awareness of our community and of our earthly destiny, but also an awareness of our common origins and common identity. It constitutes unity in multiplicity in the biological and psychological as well as the cultural spheres. By rooting our consciousness in our belonging to the Earth-Homeland, we can develop a sense of responsibility and mutual solidarity, and civilize human relationships in all parts of the globe.

A new way of thinking is closely linked with a new consciousness. This does not mean that we have to "unalienate" ourselves (to some extent we have to alienate ourselves from others to become ourselves); rather, it means that we have to disabuse ourselves of egocentrism and ethnocentrism while safeguarding our roots.

Ignazio Masulli . . . on species consciousness

We are called upon to take a step, historically unprecedented, one that cannot even be envisaged except through the attainment of a new phase of historical consciousness—a consciousness of ourselves as a species. Today even life and the perpetuation of life have become problems of historical dimensions. The responsibility for evolution can no longer be left to the individual's instinctive defense mechanisms, which are presently the sole foundations of our value judgments. This responsibility has become a problem of historical decisions that involve the entire species.

Throughout much of its history, the evolution of the human species has gone hand in hand with attempts by society to defend itself against contingencies arising from natural calamities, as well as from threats originating in its internal environment. This has brought to the fore the forces of egotism, expressed in acts of domination and antagonism. The landscape of history is littered with unmistakable evidence of fiercely competitive behaviors in the form of weapons, fortifications, frontiers, all manner of instruments and symbols of power. Corresponding to these, in a nonmaterial guise, we find the no less rigid demarcations perpetrated by symbols of identity, sometimes superimposed on one another: the individual, the clan, the ethnic group, the nation, the race.

Today these barriers and discriminations have become walls that imprison us. Given the current world problems with their global interdependences, all our will and energy will be required if we are to break down the walls we have been erecting around and within ourselves.

It is relevant here to recall Jonas Salk's warning: Our future evolution will not be decided by the survival of the strongest but by the survival of the wisest. An essential anthropological drive, that of Being, must prevail over the pressures of the Ego. This is the transformation we are now called upon to undertake. Ervin Laszlo could hardly be clearer on this matter. I shall only emphasize three points here.

The first of these bears on the global nature of the problems facing us. Recent years have witnessed a large number of studies and debates, from institutional as well as other sources, regarding the critical disequilibrium caused by our exploitation and waste of natural resources, the demographic explosion, impacting above all the poorest areas of the world, and the growing and ever more serious divide between wealth and poverty. And who among us has not experienced a sense of frustration, even outright pessimism, feeling that all the words expended on these subjects are scarcely likely to be followed by concrete action? What emerges from the pages of this book is its global vision. This is not merely a matter of placing one problem beside another. Rather, that vision derives from the ability to trace the problems back to their historical origins; that is, to the thought and action by which they were generated. From such a standpoint, it is possible to envisage feasible solutions.

The second element, intimately connected with the first, is that Laszlo identifies the key points on which to act in order to achieve a new perspective. He speaks very clearly: The responses to the problems cannot be delegated to the traditional elite, whether economic, political, scientific, or other. They can only spring from a new consciousness, increasingly deep and embracing, which is to become the common property of the world's peoples. He states explicitly that although numerous innovative views for tackling problems of this kind have been produced by individuals and groups—though these are in a minority in the science community—they remain too far removed from public opinion. The new approaches are not made intelligible to the public, and the widely diffused conceptions have tended to become obsolete.

I might add that the diffusion of innovative views and approaches impacting on the consciousness of the majority entails a change in the relationship between science and society. No less significant is the warning to the economic and political elite that unless we rethink the ethics of economics and politics it will be impossible to obtain a different relationship between the power-holders and those affected by them. Room must be found for decisions that are not dictated by vested and regional interests. Inasmuch as we are required to make choices different from those that have gone before, our decisions must be directed toward the general objectives of humankind as a whole. This will only be possible if we recognize the truly fundamental requirements.

A third point concerns the quest for the sources of the new Holos consciousness. In this regard, art and science are linked anew. Art is implicated because it is capable of plumbing the depth of the significance of the human condition and of the relationships that bind people with one another and to the living world as a whole. Science is implicated because it contributes toward recovering a unitary meaning of the world. These potentials of art and science need focused attention and careful development. The scientific revolution of the seventeenth century prepared the way for the amazing scientific and technical advances of our time, but it adopted instrumental and regional ways of thinking. It is the historical task of contemporary scientists to rebuild a unitary, organic conception of reality.

Gary Zukav . . . on the unprecedented evolutionary transformation

The human species has entered a period of profound, fundamental, and unprecedented change. Its perceptual capability is expanding beyond the five senses. It is acquiring the ability to see itself as part of a larger fabric of life. The universe is becoming visible to it as a spiritual enterprise rather than a material one.

Until recently, humankind has been limited in its perception to the five senses and has evolved through the exploration of the physical world. The new, emerging humanity is not limited to the perception of the five senses. It is highly intuitive, and its means of evolution is entirely different. The emerging humanity evolves through responsible choice. A responsible choice is a choice that produces consequences for which the chooser is willing to assume responsibility.

This changes everything. First, the perception of power is changing from the ability to manipulate and control to the alignment of the personality with the soul. Multisensory humans see themselves as more than minds and bodies. They see themselves as immortal souls evolving voluntarily in a special learning environment: the domain of the five senses. The perception of power as the ability to manipulate and control is neither appealing nor accurate to them. They see alignment of the personality with the soul as authentic power and responsible choice as the means of creating it. The evolutionary modality of the emerging humankind is the alignment of the personality with the soul through responsible choice.

Social activism apart from the creation of authentic power is the pursuit of external power—the attempt to impose one will upon another. The pursuit of external power produces only violence and destruction. What once served the evolution of humankind is now counterproductive and dangerous. Old ways of responding to the challenges of a life on Earth no longer work. The challenges have never been greater or more numerous: deteriorating control of nuclear weapons, massive pollution, rapid extinction of species and cultures, increasing violence, a longer human life span, and an exponentially increasing human population with a finite resource base to support it.

The old ways are manipulation and control with the assistance of the intellect. The new ways—and the only ones that now offer humankind a future—are responsible choices of harmony, cooperation, sharing, and reverence for life with the assistance of the heart.

Any cause that identifies a villain contributes to the problem, not to its solution. The problem is internal; only its ramifications are external. The external mirrors the internal. No effort to change the reflection will change the source of the reflection. No war to end wars will end war, nor ever has. No campaign against greed will end avarice unless it is waged where the greed lives—in the heart of the campaigner. Every change requires a change in consciousness. This has always been the case. Now humankind is developing the ability to recognize and cooperate with this dynamic.

This is the unprecedented evolutionary transformation that is under way: the expansion of human consideration beyond its own needs into the limitless universe of wisdom and compassion of which it is part. It is our emerging ability to collaborate, for the first time as a species, with nonphysical yet real forms of life that are in advance of our own. It is partnering with the universe in the most conscious and responsible ways and the joy and fulfillment that result. It is radical personal responsibility for the whole through self-cultivation of compassion and kindness, through the pursuit of authentic power. At the heart of this endeavor is cultivation of the consciousness that is required. This is for each individual to undertake and complete. It is the greatest challenge and joy that now fills our lives.

The Partners Comment

Franz-Josef Radermacher—Director, Initiative for a Global Marshall Plan (Germany)

With this new book, Ervin Laszlo, president of the Club of Budapest, makes an important contribution to the understanding of the present global situation. Laszlo, the Club of Budapest, the World Wisdom Council, and other think tanks such as the Club of Rome, the Eco-Social Forum of Europe, the Foundation for Global Contract, and the Initiative for a Global Marshall Plan all deal with the world *problematique*, and argue that our world is presently in an extremely difficult situation; trends are going in the wrong direction. This is not the path to sustainability; this is a path to social gaps, poverty, cultural imbalance, terror, war, and destruction. Recent terrorist attacks, the flood disaster in New Orleans, and the war in Iraq give an indication that things are going in the wrong direction.

Note, however, that we are in trouble not because science is not powerful enough or our technological means are not sufficient in scope and in variety. No, it is because we use our ideas in the wrong way, driven as we are by global frameworks that contradict all the experiences we have in regard to how to organize systems that work. Some powerful groups have succeeded in implementing a global regime of selective free trade that is attractive to people and organizations in positions of power, but that stress nature as well as the majority of people on the globe. This is bound to lead to disaster and to conflict.

But whether we will pursue this path to the end or choose a more enlightened path has not been decided yet. Getting on a more enlightened path is not a problem in principle. What we need is a different way of thinking, based on the experience of successful states. A more enlightened philosophy is illustrated in the expansion process of the European Community, a model of globalization that may be the only one today that works.

Ervin Laszlo describes the situation convincingly. What is at stake, and what are the alternatives? With reference to systems and chaos theory, he describes what it means to have reached a critical phase of bifurcation—a Chaos Point. We are close to this tipping point, and that means that the things we do—that each individual does—can make a difference. It is at the decision-window prior to the tipping point that the activities of small groups and even of individuals become of the utmost importance.

There is a chance that thousands will soon act, because the prospect of the coming disaster makes them aware of the need for it. This is like the wave in front of a boat that signals to everyone who sees it that something "big" is coming. Today, the visible signs of the coming disaster are migration, starvation, climate change, natural catastrophe, limits to resources, and excessive pollution. The best prospect of reaching a critical tipping point is to coordinate millions of people who individually all take small steps, but if their steps are enlightened and mutually reinforcing they become the wave that changes the world.

Ervin Laszlo is certainly one who gives us hope, who motivates change, who works towards making use of the tipping point for choosing the right path to the future. His book joins others that address this topic, but it makes its own contribution in particular in working out the elements and the dimensions of chaos in the transformation. Laszlo takes still another step forward in uniting the search for the way toward a better future with the findings of his own prior research regarding connections between people, and between people and nature.

I wish this book many, many readers who then become an active part of the tipping point that can take us to a better future.

James O'Dea— Past President, Institute of Noetic Sciences (California)

Two facts define and shape the human experience:

- we are living creatures embedded in a biosphere and enmeshed in a complex web of life;
- we have an inner life which derives its vivid existence from making meaning.

Whether you argue that we are essentially spiritual beings having a biological experience for the purpose of our soul's growth, that we emerge from and are sustained by a field of consciousness which is antecedent to biological life, or whether you believe that our self-reflective awareness emerged out of the primordial slime and is a by-product of evolutionary complexity, we can all agree that *human beings are biological creatures who require meaning in their lives as much as the oxygen they breathe and the nutrients they put in their bodies.*

The problem, as we now see at the dawn of the twenty-first century, is that we as a species appear to be overwhelmed by our inability to bring these two facts of our existence into a coherent and harmonious relationship. In fact these two fundamental aspects of human life appear to be increasingly at war with each other, precipitating whole systems crises and ratcheting up credible scenarios that question our long-term survival.

So how did our exquisite capacity to make meaning get so out of alignment with the biological requirements for living sustainably on planet Earth? How did prevailing meanings get so ahead of us that they will destroy us unless we transform them? Why is nature so devalued while excessive value is placed on machines and their myriad functions?

The long answer involves an analysis that seeks to unpack the reasons why materialism has become the dominant organizing principle across the world, decimating with ever-increasing velocity the subtlety, beauty, and diversity of cultures, crafts and trades, landscapes, and untold numbers of species and increasingly jeopardizing the quality of air, food, and water. It involves an analysis of the mind-body split, the mind-matter split, the rift with the natural order and nature's rhythms, and the purported role a host of philosophers and scientists have had in shaping the dominant scientific materialism, systemic economic inequities, and persistent violence in the world today. It also involves an analysis of how meaning organizes itself and conditions our awareness, creating highly selective filters and blind spots. Finally, the long answer involves the best understanding available to us about the nature and source of consciousness and its capacity to transform dysfunctional and outmoded meaning systems, and their derivative behaviors.

The short answer to the question—how did we get so far ahead of ourselves that we now threaten our own health, well-being, and even survival?—is ego.

Ego has also been the subject of much analysis since humans first demonstrated an ability to cultivate wisdom. Throughout the ages, it has been pointed out that ego must be transcended. But ego finds it profoundly confusing to appreciate that its role is limited and transitory and it pushes back at both individual and collective levels with negative consequences. Enormous suffering stems from our inability to grasp the function of ego, which is to cocoon enough self-awareness to catalyze transformation from one state of being to another. Instead of being the shell from which we hatch to higher consciousness, it becomes the self-illusioning prison described so beautifully in ancient spiritual texts. It becomes the barrier to higher development and it obstructs transformation. What ego values so dearly must be released for something of greater value that it cannot perceive and in favor of a more inclusive meaning that it cannot comprehend!

This lineup of concepts around meaning, values, ego, and stages of development has consequences for individual, social, and global transformation.

Meaning constellates around values. What we value has become a predictor of what we will buy, how much we will consume, how we will vote, who we will relate to and who not, and to almost every manifestation of private and social behavior and belief. All across the globe, values have become a red-hot issue. Value-meaning clusters have received much scrutiny, from developmental psychologists to sociologists, from entrepreneurs to political strategists. Our values are sought after, interpreted, manipulated, debated, challenged, harangued, and even been the basis for violent conflict, terrorism, and war.

After the Second World War, the nations of the world came together and created with a profound degree of consensus the Universal Declaration of Human Rights. The carnage and destruction of war across the world precipitated a resolve to seek higher ground. Thus, this groundbreaking document proclaimed the value of all human beings and affirmed their rights as never before. The history of human rights has been one marked by ever-increasing inclusions: rights that had not been afforded to women, children, minority populations, refugees, the physically and mentally challenged, and those of differing sexual orientation have gradually been added. The right of every person to basic health, education, security, and due legal process has steadily increased. Out of the trauma of global conflagration, the imperative to surrender lesser values to greater universal values was forged with visionary power and universally positive consequences.

There is some agreement that values and meaning cluster in stages from rudimentary order and discipline to universal conscience, from basic food and safety needs to self-actualization, from small self-protecting clans to universally oriented service. A worldview which synthesizes beliefs, values, and meaning at various stages of development brings coherence to that phase as long as it holds together. Then new insight, information, or ways of being challenge the existing structure of belief significantly enough to push it to a new phase. This process is always more than linear change, it is transformational. Changes in popular opinion and fashion (the subject of endless market research) are linear changes; they change only surface appearances and do not shift levels and paradigms. Transformation is the process which facilitates the movement from limiting and constricting forms of identification to something larger, more inclusive, and more whole.

Now our day has come. The day when we step out beyond the narrower imagination of nation states to call for their inclusion in a bold collaboration for all life: a collaboration that was once the dream of idealists is now the call of an awakened realism, awakened by the realization that the next phase change is an imperative. This phase shift has been likened to a collective species transition from adolescence to maturity: In coming to terms with the reality of limits, we enter the fullness of our creative power.

We will have to give up some of our toys! We will have to assume more responsibility, with a knowledge that the skies, the oceans, the forests, and all the life they contain are woven inextricably into the quality of our lives and all life to come. We will have to learn to live and dialogue with different viewpoints and perspectives. We will have to share.

And supporting our collective shift from adolescence to maturity is a science that itself is coming of age. It is a science that brings fresh insight from exploring the roots of human consciousness. It tells us, based on much good research, that we are made for love, nurturing relationships, gratefulness, forgiveness, altruism, and even laughter. It tells that resentment, unforgiving behavior, persistent anger, anxiety, and isolation compound negative energy, which damages our health, breaks up relationships, and triggers violence. It tells us that we have healing capacities and that our thoughts extend into the sensate world. This is not moral prescript about vice and virtue; this is integral science, the science that looks at both the inner being and external phenomena. Through this science now we know so much more about the causal relationship between ideas, attitudes, emotions, perceptions, intentions, beliefs, and what we see manifest in the world. We are even steadily advancing towards theories of quantum entanglement and consciousness that may utterly transform our notion of the relationship between the individual and the collective.

Integral science explores the optimal development of our inner lives and capacities and the translation of subjective human awareness and creativity into enlightened systems. It is a science of bringing the outer and the inner into alignment. It brings worlds together that now seem perilously disconnected. It scans more deeply the very nature of our being, explores the deep structure and design of the universe, and the most adequate and fulfilling designs for living. It confirms that humans exist in a spacious consciousness whose limits are unknown, as well as in an interconnected and richly sensorial reality that in turn profoundly affects their health and well-being. It is fascinated by the degree to which the subjective world of our experience influences and interacts with the world of frequencies, energy, space, time, and matter.

To match this integral science we must dare to catalyze an integral education that will tap into the inner reaches of the coming generations, nurture expanded awareness of human wholeness, and unleash the creativity that is so needed to transform our world. And integral medicine is just beginning to emerge, with its expanded vision and practice around wholeness and healing. Integral businesses are also coming onto the scene, defining success in terms of ecological benefits, socially responsible values, and the well-being of employees. Integral politics seems a distant dream in which politicians will really compete to serve the greatest ecological, social, and global good; when politicians will be appointed because they are skilled transformational agents whose values and maturity are demonstrably not ego based.

And so the rising tide of transformation that is now called for is percolating in the hearts and minds of people across the world—for to truly be the transformation we are referring to it cannot be some new colonial or missionary enterprise. It must come from within a spiritual passion that is inspired by unity. It must be a response to a primitively felt need and come from a place inside that knows directly what is in the best interest of the whole. It must rise in collective consciousness, and it must be expressed and embodied. It is not a mental transformation but one which resonates all the way through spirit, mind, and body. This is a transformation that first exposes those lies which are a complete mismatch between what is professed and what is acted upon; it has to do so in order to secure the ground for a much fuller truth and greater integrity. Be careful, for it is a time when, for each one of us, thought, word, and deed need to be in coherent alignment or inconsistencies will become painfully apparent.

Will we transform in time?

Find someone's hand, and then another and another. Don't concern yourself with the age, race, gender, or social status of those you reach out to; just trust your instincts. Ask each other what you truly value most and what you are willing to let go in order to be in full alignment with whatever is most precious to us all. Remember, meaning is a great organizer which configures and gains great momentum around our values. What millions of people are beginning to feel deep in their hearts may very well be tomorrow's headlines. This won't occur if your heart is numbed or your head is in a trance; there's just no pretending when it comes to a transformation of this order.

When you have taken the leap, you will be so happy that you have eyes to see, hands to touch, and heart to feel the beauty of a world transformed.

And if you don't, I won't be around either. This is the real significance of the Chaos Point described by Ervin Laszlo in this book. And when you have read this book, you will understand that I am deeply invested in our taking this leap together.

Hiroo Saionji, President, and Masami Saionji, Chairperson, the Goi Peace Foundation (Japan)

This important new book by Ervin Laszlo, founder of systems philosophy and general evolution theory, comes at an extremely critical juncture in the evolution of humankind. Our civilization stands at a crossroads at this very moment. We have been feeling growing uneasiness over an impending crisis in the environment, in ethnic and religious struggles, in aggression and terrorism, and in the potential use of nuclear weapons. At the basis of all these crises looms a serious crisis in human consciousness.

Human consciousness is a creative force. Because we have paid so little attention to how we are directing our own consciousness, we human beings have propelled the world along a dangerous path. Now, disastrous results are erupting all around us. The world has become economically, socially, and ecologically unsustainable, and human civilization itself is at stake. Many people feel fearful and confused and powerless about their future. How did we create this situation? How can we change directions? To answer these questions we need to look deeply into our own consciousness and behold our own values and beliefs.

Throughout the twentieth century, what did we human beings value? For the most part, we valued material things, and strove to create materially affluent lives for ourselves. We focused all our efforts and energy into development and production, promoting lifestyles governed by speed, greed, and consumerism. While this preoccupation with materially oriented aims and values fostered a great expansion in material civilization, it has created a mountain of global problems and the unsustainable world in which we find ourselves today.

We have persistently believed that we have enemies. We harbored conflict and disharmony in our mind, such as good versus evil, health versus illness, life versus death, wealth versus poverty, and self versus God. Because we believed that we had enemies, our life-energy polarized the world. Today, we are still struggling to defeat the enemies we created in our own consciousness. The war against crime, the war against terrorism, the war against poverty, the war against disease—struggles like these are bound to continue for as long as human beings continue to perceive life as a never-ending struggle between opposing forces.

If we want to reverse this situation, we must first and foremost rid our own heart of conflict and divisiveness. Only when we are able to achieve wholeness and healing in our own self will we be able to achieve peace and harmony in the world.

In *The Chaos Point,* Ervin Laszlo alerts us to the enormous potential that each of us possesses for freeing ourselves of our erroneous beliefs. As he rightly points out, we are living in a unique time when each human being can create a great evolutionary shift in human consciousness.

Inner awakening and the emergence of creativity in individuals are the forces that will shape our collective future. If we raise our consciousness to a higher level and experience the interconnectedness of all life, our behaviors and priorities will change drastically. The frontier sciences can play an important role in this regard, by giving rise to new views of the world and a new understanding of life.

Indeed, the crisis we face today is at the same time an unprecedented opportunity to make a major leap in the evolution of humankind. There are numerous innovative initiatives and creative activities emerging around the world to facilitate the transformation of civilization. Now more than ever, each of us is called upon to become a proactive agent for positive change.

The Goi Peace Foundation considers it its mission to build cooperation among individuals and organizations in all fields in the interest of achieving the shared goal of peace on Earth. We are committed to working in partnership with likeminded organizations such as the Club of Budapest, the Club of Rome, the World Wisdom Council, the Global Marshall Plan Initiative, and the Universal Forum of Cultures of Monterrey so that humanity can safely transit the current decision-window and in reaching the Chaos Point tip the evolution of our world toward a civilization of respect, harmony, and oneness.

Ashok Gangadean, Founder-Director, Global Dialogue Institute, and Co-Convenor, World Commission on Global Consciousness and Spirituality

All through the ages we have had prophesies, visions, and predictions of our world coming to an end. Our biblical context, for example, gives us revelations of an apocalyptic end in its unfolding providential drama of Divine Justice and eschatology. Various indigenous calendars converge on the coming decade as a crucial transitioning for the human condition and our life on Earth. And in recent decades with an expanding awareness of megatrends and patterns on a planetary scale, we became acquainted with a number of urgent warnings of unprecedented ecological, economic, ideological, and political crises that threaten the sustainability of our world, and our very survival on this planet.

There is a growing sense in a number of circles that the fuse is short and that if we do not make dramatic changes now it may be too late to turn things around. What are we to believe? Is our world as we know it about to come to an end? Are we now at a critical moment in our evolution that is do or die? Is there an objective validity to the diagnosis that we are in the midst of a monumental crisis that will determine our destiny?

In *The Chaos Point: The World at the Crossroads* Ervin Laszlo takes a decisive stand on this issue. He builds on insights from earlier works, *Macroshift* (2001), *You Can Change the World* (2003) and *Science and the Reenchantment of the Cosmos* (2006), and brings out clearly that we have reached a critical turning point where we face crossroads and choices that will determine our fate. He sees this "Chaos Point" as one where we face the specter of global collapse, but also the opportunity for a renewal of global proportions.

Laszlo suggests that in the next few years humanity faces crucial decisions and choices to turn around unsustainable megatrends that bring us to the threshold of a tipping point beyond which there can be no return. As he sees it, we must either consciously evolve to a sustainable civilization in which the whole human family may co-exist in a more secure, flourishing, and peaceful way, or else face a terrible scenario in which there is an unprecedented implosion of our social, economic, political, and ecological systems. Laszlo's message is that it is up to us to envision and co-create this new world. He suggests that each of us has the power and the potential to play a decisive role.

My own journey as a philosopher over the past four decades has brought me to a remarkable convergence with Laszlo's view of the present human condition. The new frontier of global thinking takes us beyond localized perspectives, traditions, worldviews, and disciplinary orientations to a higher-order rational space, a higher dimension of rationality and integral science that discloses astounding planetary patterns. When we adventure into this global horizon we discover a long-emerging tradition of vision and wisdom that grounds, corroborates, and validates the deep diagnosis of the present planetary crisis uncovered and uniquely narrated by Laszlo.

In order to understand the true nature of the planetary crisis we now face we need to stand back and gain critical distance from our localized perspectives, worldviews, ideologies, and disciplinary orientations. When we break the powerful circuits of our usually overpowering worldviews and make the dimensional shift in consciousness into the more expansive space where our diverse worldviews, cultures, and disciplines co-arise, our minds are dilated and a global lens opens that is inter-perspectival. In this expanded higher order perspective astounding patterns become evident in the evolution of the human condition.

The diverse crises we face on the planet today are the cumulative result of individual and collective minding practices through the ages. From the integral perspective of the global lens it becomes clear that the compounded effects of egomentalism have brought us to the current untenable and unsustainable world. But it also becomes clear that the cumulative effect of the awakening forces of consciousness is also growing in momentum as a counter-force to the fragmenting and disintegral forces of egocentric minding.

To truly see the enormity of the great drama we are now living through we need the long-range integral aperture of global vision and wisdom. The powers of the global lens enable us to connect the dots, make significant connections and discern mega-patterns that are not available to the disconnective and disintegral habits of egomentalism. Visionaries such as Laszlo, who have the capacity to connect the dots and discern the workings of whole systems, are able to see what has been overlooked through ego-eyes and is now urgently before us. In this perspective it is apparent that the egomental cultures have run their course, are dysfunctional, in decay and disintegration, and are facing their evolutionary and historical termination. As a critical mass of humans on this planet awakens and rises to global minding, the dysfunctional patterns of egomentalism will be inevitably left behind. The challenge for the awakening global citizen is to undertake the unprecedented self-organization, networking, and community building so as to co-create a mass of awakened humans of sufficient proportion to turn around the current destructive megatrends.

The stakes are high: our survival on this planet is in question. The egomental forces are peaking and reaching the "tipping point" even as the counter forces of integral awakening are reaching an unprecedented ignition point. It appears that more and more people are sensing in an exponential way that the old habits and practices are taking us down the wrong path, and are ready to advance to higher ground.

Clearly, at this moment in our evolution we face grave dangers. But this crisis is also a threshold of amazing new possibilities where everything is to be gained. We have a choice when we are clear about what is coming down, and how we can change the world with new patterns of minding. The main crisis of our time is a crisis of consciousness. When we rise together in integral consciousness, we have the opportunity to bring forth sustainable cultures and a sustainable world. A new planetary civilization awaits.

When we examine our current world situation through the integral vision of the global lens, we perceive the scope, validity, and contextual grounding of Laszlo's deep diagnosis and prescription. The historic power, urgency, and significance of his work become evident. We are in the midst of a planetary crisis that calls forth unprecedented individual and collective global awakening; we are at a "decision window." Our collective survival is in danger if we do not wake up, pay attention, and realize our enormous power of choice, taking action with wisdom, foresight, and courage.

The above realization is the *raison d'être* of several of our initiatives in regard to a new planetary civilization. The World Commission on Global Consciousness and Spirituality, the Club of Budapest, the World Wisdom Council, and allied initiatives like the Global Marshall Plan, the Goi Peace Foundation, and the Universal Forum of Cultures of Monterrey are essentially focused on tending the crisis of consciousness before us and facilitating the shift to an awakened planetary civilization.

With his global vision Laszlo helps us to get a deeper understanding of the historic crisis we are now facing. The clearer we are about this crisis the more effective we can be in responding to it. Our future turns on this.

About the Club of Budapest, and the Documents of the Club of Budapest

The Club of Budapest is an informal association of creative people in diverse fields of human creativity: art, literature, the spiritual domains, as well as the business world and civil society at large. It is dedicated to the proposition that only by changing ourselves can we change our world, and that to change ourselves we need keen insight and genuine creativity. The members of the Club of Budapest use their creativity and insight to enhance awareness of global problems and human opportunities. They communicate their views in word and image, in sound and motion, and in the myriad new media and technologies. They are recognized world leaders in their fields; their names are assurance of insight, and their membership a testimony of their dedication to our common future.

The Challenge and the Mission

The insight in view of which the Club of Budapest has been founded is that today's world is an interconnected whole where what one person does affects all. This world is in rapid and fundamental transformation. The outcome of the transformation is as yet open. Thus our future is not to be predicted; it must be created. The possibilities are vast, and the choice among them is ours. The new worlds we could create range from an inhuman world of frustration, conflict, and violence to a world of peace and equity, capable of offering conditions for personal fulfillment and social development. The world we will create in reality depends on us. It depends on the thinking, values, and perceptions of people in all walks of life, in all parts of the world. The alternative to a world governed "from above" can only be a self-governing world, one that chooses the shape of things to come "from within." The critical factor in the choice of our common destiny is the thinking, the valuing, and the perception of creative people in all walks of life. It is the shape of our individual and collective consciousness.

Nobody can shape our consciousness but ourselves. To evolve the kind of consciousness that could ensure that our future is bright, we must apprehend our situation on this planet in all its dimensions—sense it with our heart and soul. Creative people in all spheres of innovative thinking and acting are the greatest resource of contemporary humanity. This resource cannot, must not, be left unharnessed in meeting the unparalleled challenge: to transform today's inequitable and unsustainable world into a humane and sustainable one.

The Club of Budapest is dedicated to the proposition that the "revolution of consciousness" is perhaps the last, and certainly the best, hope of humankind. The club is dedicated to harnessing the power of creativity of artists, writers, leaders in business and in civil society, and innovators in all spheres of human activity to catalyze this peaceful and vital revolution in the shared interest of our generation and of generations to come.

The Manifesto on Planetary Consciousness

A new way of thinking has become the necessary condition for responsible living and acting. Evolving it means fostering creativity in all people, in all parts of the world. Creativity is not a genetic but a cultural endowment of human beings. Culture and society change fast, while genes change slowly: No more than one-half of one percent of the human genetic endowment is likely to alter in an entire century. Hence most of our genes date from the Stone Age or before; they could help us to live in the jungles of nature but not in the jungles of civilization. Today's economic, social, and technological environment is our own creation, and only the creativity of our mind—our culture, spirit, and consciousness—will enable us to cope with it. Genuine creativity does not remain paralyzed when faced with unusual and unexpected problems, but confronts them openly, without prejudice. Cultivating creativity is a precondition of finding our way toward a globally interconnected society in which individuals, enterprises, states, and the whole family of peoples and nations can live together peacefully, cooperatively, and with mutual benefit.

A Call for Responsibility

In the course of the past several decades, people in many parts of the world have become conscious of their rights as well as of many persistent violations of them. This development is important, but in itself it is not enough. We must now become conscious of the factor without which neither rights nor other values can be effectively safeguarded: our individual and collective responsibilities. We are not likely to grow into a peaceful and cooperative human family unless we become responsible social, economic, political, and cultural actors.

We human beings need more than food, water, and shelter—more even than remunerated work, self-esteem, and social acceptance. We also need something to live for: an ideal to achieve, a responsibility to accept. Because we are aware of the consequences of our actions, we can and must accept responsibility for them. Such responsibility goes deeper than many of us may think. In today's world, all people, no matter where they live and what they do, have become responsible for their actions as:

- Private individuals
- Citizens of a country
- Collaborators in business and the economy
- Members of the human community
- Persons endowed with mind and consciousness

As individuals, we are responsible for seeking our interests in harmony with, and not at the expense of, the interests and well-being of others; responsible for condemning and averting any form of killing and brutality; responsible for not bringing more children into the world than we truly need and can support; and for respecting the right to life, development, and equal status and dignity of all the children, women, and men who inhabit the Earth.

As citizens of our country, we are responsible for demanding that our leaders "beat swords into plowshares" and relate to other nations peacefully and in a spirit of cooperation; that they recognize the legitimate aspirations of all communities in the human family; and that they do not abuse sovereign powers to manipulate people and the environment for shortsighted and selfish ends.

As collaborators in business and actors in the economy, we are responsible for ensuring that corporate objectives do not center uniquely on profit and growth, but include a concern that products and services respond to human needs and demands without harming people and impairing nature; that they do not serve destructive ends and unscrupulous designs; and that they respect the rights of all entrepreneurs and enterprises that compete fairly in the global marketplace.

As members of the human community, it is our responsibility to adopt a culture of nonviolence, solidarity, and economic, political, and social equality, promoting mutual understanding and respect among people and nations whether they are like us or different, demanding that all people everywhere should be empowered to respond to the challenges that face them with the material as well as spiritual resources that are required for this unprecedented task.

And as persons endowed with mind and consciousness, our responsibility is to encourage comprehension and appreciation of the excellence of the human spirit in all its manifestations, and to inspire awe and wonder for a cosmos that brought forth life and consciousness and holds out the possibility of its continued evolution toward ever higher levels of insight, understanding, love, and compassion.

A Call for Planetary Consciousness

In most parts of the world, the real potential of human beings is sadly underdeveloped. The way children are raised depresses their faculties for learning and creativity; the way young people experience the struggle for material survival results in frustration and resentment. In adults, this leads to a variety of compensatory, addictive, and compulsive behaviors. The result is the persistence of social and political oppression, economic warfare, cultural intolerance, crime, and disregard for the environment.

Eliminating social and economic ills and frustrations calls for considerable socioeconomic development, and that is not possible without better education, information, and communication. These, however, are blocked by the absence of socioeconomic development, so that a vicious cycle is produced: underdevelopment creates frustration, and frustration, giving rise to defective behaviors, blocks development. This cycle must be broken at its point of greatest flexibility and that is the development of the spirit and consciousness of human beings. Achieving this objective does not preempt the need for socioeconomic development with all its financial and technical resources, but calls for a parallel mission in the spiritual field. Unless people's spirit and consciousness evolve to the planetary dimension, the processes that stress the globalized society-nature system will intensify and create a shock wave that could jeopardize the entire transition toward a peaceful and cooperative global society. This would be a setback for humanity and a danger for everyone. Evolving human spirit and consciousness is the first vital cause shared by the whole of the human family.

Planetary consciousness is knowing as well as feeling the vital interdependence and essential oneness of humankind and the conscious adoption of the ethic and the ethos that this entails. Its evolution is the basic imperative of human survival on this planet.

Statement on War

War is a uniquely human phenomenon: No other species kills massively its own kind. Such killing was never justified, but it had a marginal warrant at a time when war was waged among neighboring groups for the acquisition of territory with natural and human resources and could be limited to the territories and the warriors of the protagonists. At a time when resources are not limited to defined territories and hostilities cannot be contained, war is neither politically nor economically justified. Given that modern warfare kills innocent civilians, inflicts serious damage on the life-supporting environment, and may escalate to a global conflagration, waging war is a crime against all of humanity. It needs to be recognized as such. No nation-state should have the legitimate right to declare war on any other nation-state.

The stockpiling of weapons of mass destruction is not a warrant for one nation-state to wage war on another. Weapons of mass destruction—whether they are nuclear, chemical, biological, or conventional—are a threat to human life and habitat by whoever possesses them. They are not tolerable in the hands of any state, whether it is large or small, rich or poor, headed by a dictator or an elected politician. Such weapons need to be eliminated from the arsenals of every single state, a task that does not call for waging war and is not the self-declared prerogative of any government but the responsibility of the global community of all peoples and states.

There will be no lasting peace on earth until weapons of mass destruction themselves are destroyed, their production and stockpiling proscribed, and strategies calling for their use replaced by strategies of dialogue, negotiation, and, if necessary, internationally agreed economic and political sanctions. *Potential aggressors and terrorists must be stopped, but war is not the way to stop them.* Fighting violence with violence is to act on the principle of an eye for an eye and a tooth for a tooth, and this (as Gandhi said) may end up making everyone blind and toothless.

The time has come for the world community to recognize that war, rather than an instrument for the elimination of terrorists and aggressors, is itself an act of aggression that threatens human life and the integrity of the environment on which human life, and all life on earth, vitally depends.

The Wise Response to Violence

The September 11 suicide attack on New York's World Trade Center and Washington's Pentagon was an offense against all of human life and every civilization. We condemn this act of terrorism and call to ethical and peace-loving people the world over to join together to put an end to terrorism and violence in all its forms. There is no solution to the world's problems in killing innocent people and destroying their workplaces and habitations.

If we are to succeed in eradicating violence and terrorism from the world, we must act wisely. Violence and terrorism will not be vanquished by retaliation on the principle of an eye for an eye and a tooth for a tooth. The ultimate roots of violence lie deeper than the fanatic commitment of terrorists and the religious claims of fundamentalists. Killing one group of terrorists will not solve the problem: As long as the roots are there, others will grow in their place.

The terror that surfaces in today's world is a symptom of long-standing and deep-seated frustrations, resentment, and perceived injustice, and eliminating the symptom does not cure the malady. The Club of Budapest is committed to searching for the causes of violence in the world. Until and unless the causes are eliminated, there will not be peace in the world, only an uncertain interlude between acts of violence and larger-scale hostilities. When people are frustrated, they harbor hate and the desire for revenge and cannot relate to each other in a spirit of peace and cooperation. Whether the cause is the wounded ego of a person or the wounded self-respect of a people, and whether it is the wish for personal revenge or a holy war for the defense of a faith, the result is violence, death, and catastrophe. Attaining peace in people's hearts is a precondition of attaining peace in the world.

The Club of Budapest maintains that the wise response to violence and terrorism is to help people to be at peace with themselves and their fellow humans near and far. Promoting solidarity and cooperation in the shared cause of fairness and justice is the only feasible path to lasting peace on Earth.

Statements of the World Wisdom Council

The Budapest Declaration: Wisdom at the Tipping Point— Shifting to New Thinking and a New Civilization

1. We, the members of the World Wisdom Council, are committed to the reversal of current trends toward chaos and destruction. We believe that the world can be constructively changed. A new civilization can be created. We call on governments, businesses, educators, artists, scientists, activists, and all concerned citizens to join their commitment to ours. We call on people in every walk of life to become aware of the critical nature of the world situation and use the power of new thinking and acting to bring about the necessary changes.

2. The wise people of all traditions have admonished us to see humanity as one family, to honor the sanctity of life and creation, to nurture love and compassion, and to apply the golden rule of treating others as we want to be treated ourselves. For the first time in history, the application of this wisdom is not only a precondition of personal growth and fulfillment, but also a precondition of human survival.

3. Neither breakdown in chaos nor breakthrough to a new civilization is fated. The future is not to be foretold; it is to be created. It can be decisively formed by every human being endowed with both consciousness and conscience. There are workable alternatives to the way we do things in the world today that could help us deflect the trends that move us toward crisis and pave the way toward a more sustainable and peaceful new civilization.

4. A basic *cause* of unsustainability is the dysfunctional and egocentric thinking that gives rise to perceptions and priorities that lead to destructive conduct. The basic *remedy* is the transformation of the prevalent mindset. In this context, "mindset" embraces rational as well as intuitive, cognitive as well as emotional elements: the full scope of human consciousness.

5. Humanity's great wisdom traditions, east and west, north and south, concur that asking fundamental questions is a vital step in the awakening of wisdom, as they help us see and experience the essential link between our consciousness and its immediate tangible effect on our lives. These questions awaken higher, more integral forms of intelligence that can initiate the solution, dissolution, and resolution of the problems we all currently face.

6. There are some fundamental questions we need to ponder. They include questions such as:

- Can we make wealth, power, and technology serve us, instead of enslave us?
- Can we have peace within and among ourselves without living at peace with nature?
- Can we have a peaceful and sustainable world without understanding how others view the world?
- Can we afford to ignore the intrinsic wisdom present in traditional cultures and present also in young children when it comes to conducting our life in modern societies?
- Must we not question whether modern practices truly bring justice to law, healing to medicine, and sustainability to the conduct of politics and business?
- Can we transform in time the prevalent glorification of greed, lust, and power into a mindset hallmarked by dedication to justice for everyone, and respect for all people whether they live in our culture and society or in others?

There are also more practical questions we should ask. For example, where is the wisdom in a system that:

- Produces weapons that are more dangerous than the conflicts they are meant to solve and substitutes a cult of violence for a culture of peace?
- Continues to undervalue women and abandons half of its children in poverty and hunger?
- Creates an overproduction of food, but fails to make it available to the hungry?
- Ignores the very principles of fairness and justice that we ask our children to follow?
- Expects individuals to abide by the golden rule of treating others as they would be treated themselves, yet ignores this elementary rule of fairness in relations among states and among businesses?
- Faces a gamut of tasks and challenges, yet puts more and more people out of work?
- Requires unrelenting economic and financial growth for it to function and not to crash?
- Faces long-term structural and operational problems, yet bases its criteria of success on short-term accounting periods and the day-to-day behavior of stock exchanges?

- Assesses social and economic progress in terms of the gross national product and leaves out of this accounting the quality of life of the people and the level of fulfillment of their basic human needs?
- Gives full priority to maximizing the productivity of labor (even though millions are unemployed or underemployed) rather than improving the productivity of resources (notwithstanding that most natural resources are finite and many are scarce and nonrenewable)?
- Fights religious fundamentalism but enshrines "market fundamentalism" (the belief that the market can right all wrongs and solve all problems)?

7. We conclude that the question is no longer *whether* a fundamental change is coming, but whether the change will be *for the better* or *for the worse, when* it will be coming, and *at what price.* The sooner we pave the way to positive change, the less traumatic will be the transformation and the smaller its human, economic, and ecological cost. All of us now share the responsibility for realizing that we live at the tipping point of contemporary civilization and for recognizing that informed thinking and responsible acting are needed to bring us to the threshold of a civilization that is truly peaceful and sustainable.

The Hanover Declaration: Global Wisdom in Action toward a New Global Civilization

1. We, the members of the World Wisdom Council, hereby reaffirm our mandate which recognizes the powerful transformative force of our collective global wisdom to address the diverse problem areas now facing humanity in the most effective way, and thus to bring forth the most powerful practical solutions to the urgent crises before us on a planetary scale. In this spirit we herein incorporate our "Budapest Declaration: Wisdom at the Tipping Point—Shifting to New Thinking and a New Civilization" and the "The Mandate of the Council," which is its preamble.

2. Furthermore, in now examining in greater depth the range of challenges and crises that threaten our collective sustainability and survival, we find that the most crucial global issue is the vital importance of recognizing that our mentality matters: that how we conduct our mind with habits of thought and patterns of consciousness is the single most powerful factor in creating our living realities. We thus reaffirm that this global axiom of our great wisdom traditions must be our highest priority in approaching and solving our diverse crises.

3. In this light, we recognize that there is global wisdom that is deeply grounded in our ancient teachings, but which has now taken us to new and unprecedented dimensions of global consciousness and integral intelligence at the frontier where the most advanced scientific thinking finds common ground with highest global spirituality. The collective wisdom of the ages discloses that Reality is a holistic, dynamic, unified field of relations wherein everything is interactive and interconnected. Egocentric patterns of consciousness directly cause chronic pathological dynamics of fragmentation, alienation, separation, polarization, and breakdown in relations, thus producing a world in which personal and cultural dysfunctions and illness of all sorts abound.

4. This global wisdom also teaches that we have a choice in how we conduct our mind and consciousness and can self-transform our mentality to more whole-some, mature, integral patterns that flow in harmony with the interconnectivity of objective Reality. This shift to a new integral mentality means a higher form of cul-ture, which embodies the teachings of global wisdom—a new global civilization based on awakened global consciousness, mindful deep dialogue, compassion, mutual respect and care, personal freedom and empowerment, and harmony and nonviolence among cultures and religions and with our living ecologies.

5. Further, the Council believes that this is the most appropriate context for situating the diverse urgent problem areas and crises facing humanity in the twenty-first century. We thus find that it is not enough to itemize, catalogue, or inventory the now well-charted list of problem areas: religious conflict, failure of global governance, human (in)security, militarization and threat of nuclear weapons, inadequate education, depletion of nonrenewable resources, global poverty and hunger, human rights abuse, environmental degradation, abuse of women and children, to name a few. Rather, we find that the range of diverse prob-lem areas are holistically and systemically interconnected and stemming from a core common primal cause, namely the fragmenting mentality that is the genera-tive source of the various dysfunctions and cultural pathologies. This deeper diag-nosis of the primary cause of our diverse crises is the most important factor in moving to the most powerful and effective solutions.

6. Accordingly, as a direct expression of the highest transformative force of global wisdom and vision, we hereby urge all planetary citizens to recognize the holistic interconnectivity and interdependence of our diverse personal and cul-tural afflictions. We must recognize the role mentality plays in causing and gener-ating these problems, and take direct personal and collective responsibility for our

conduct of mind and the role we wittingly or unwittingly play in contributing to our planetary problems. We thereby become fully empowered as planetary citizens who can make a direct difference in transforming the mentality and habits of heart and mind that produce our afflictions. We become qualified to join forces across all our borders to cocreate a resonant energy field of a new humanity embodying the global consciousness that will solve our crises at their very source and give rise to a new global civilization.

7. Thus, this dimensional shift in mentality that has been long prescribed by our great wisdom traditions may creatively solve at their source the most chronic and intractable crises that afflict our human condition:

- Problems of religious conflict and violence may be solved through the implementing of patterns of genuine deep dialogue between religious worlds—a global dialogue between diverse faiths.
- Chronic dysfunctions in education may be corrected through the creative shifts to higher patterns of integral education, which educate the whole child as a sacred being.
- Ongoing patterns of militarization and weaponization that create chronic human insecurity may be replaced by more sane policies and practices that are based on the wisdom of human security.
- The patterns of violence that cause the abuse of human rights, violence to women and children, and all forms of human violence are addressed at their source in overcoming the egocentric and fragmenting mentality that objectifies humans and generates such abuse.

8. In this light, the Council recognizes that the individual and collective embodiment of our global wisdom in the emergence of a new civil society will be the most powerful force of global governance. We recognize that the logic of global wisdom implies strategically that the highest priority for bringing about this mass change in mentality and consciousness is to focus on transforming our primary instruments of cultural reproduction—namely, our educational institutions and practices, including parenting and enculturation of our youth. The envisioned shift to the new planetary culture and civilization should take as its highest priority the appropriate renovation and transformation of all areas of education and learning as well as the creation of new learning environments, focusing on the empowerment of youth.

The Tokyo Declaration

We, the Members of the World Wisdom Council, building on our Declarations of Budapest and Hanover in advancing our mission and fulfilling our mandate, find that

WHEREAS, humanity now faces an unprecedented opportunity for dialogue, worldwide understanding, and renewal since global crises, accelerating dysfunctional trends, and patterns in all aspects of life threaten our sustainability and very existence on this planet;

That these diverse trends and patterns have reached a dangerous tipping point that may precipitate in the coming years a catastrophic collapse and implosion of our economic, political, social, ecological, and cultural structures and institutions;

That the crises catalyzed by these trends and patterns are systemically interconnected and are the cumulative effect of chronically dysfunctional ways of thinking, outdated values, and obsolete beliefs that have dominated human life for the past several generations;

That humankind's collective wisdom through the ages makes clear that the kind of world we live in is a direct consequence of our mentality and so that to truly change our world we must transform the dominant mentality of the current civilization;

That, accordingly, the diverse crises we now face are at their core a crisis of consciousness, and thus the most powerful and effective way to transform the still dominant civilization is to address and redress the root causes, creating a timely transformation of the mentalities and patterns of consciousness that produced it;

That, further, the creative forces of human wisdom and vision have also been at work in the life of people across the planet and have been the primary engine of important advances in evolving the human condition, in particular of advancing the ethical values, spirituality, and political, social, economic, scientific, artistic, technological, educational, and other innovations that serve the betterment of humanity;

And that, in consequence, the creative consciousness-evolving forces throughout our social and cultural development exercise a cumulative effect in countering the destructive mentalities and forms of consciousness that have brought us to the current critical point, and bring humanity to the threshold of a great planetary awakening;

That, finally, in light of the realization that nothing less than the positive transformational forces in our culture can stem the tide of the destructive trends and patterns of the dominant civilization and get to the root causes of the economic, social, and ecological crises that now threaten human well-being, prosperity, and survival—

BE IT RESOLVED

That we shall henceforth make it our highest priority to do all in our power to activate and ignite the imminent, and rapidly emerging, evolved consciousness in the life of the people on a planetary scale, so as to facilitate and accelerate the blossoming of a higher form of civilization that embodies the global wisdom of humankind, in order that generations now living may bring forth a world in which the entire human family may flourish in harmony with all of nature on this precious planet;

That, to this end, we shall concentrate our efforts in building powerful and sustainable networks, co-creative partnerships, seeking to activate and draw together in common cause the vast and growing diversity of initiatives now working around the planet to bring forth a newly awakened peaceful and sustainable civilization;

That the above resolutions are to focus on calling forth a critical mass of ens, building a global community of empowered people, tapping the enormous potential of our youth, of women, and people of all ages who recognize the unprecedented global crisis and opportunity we now face, and are ready through their awakened and empowered consciousness to take personal responsibility for their own thinking, their own values, and mentality, making mindful choices in confronting and transforming the currently threatening unsustainable trends originating from obsolete forms of thinking, values, and consciousness;

And, as a highest urgency, to use the mass media, the power of the Internet and the digital multimedia, as well as all appropriate forms of communication to build a global network of solidarity so as to co-create a critical mass of awakened citizens and activate the creative resonant energy of mass consciousness that is essential to overcome the inertia of complacency, fear, and paralyzing pessimism and turn the course of humanity toward a new planetary civilization as a concrete, living reality;

With this objective in mind, today, in Tokyo as we launch a partnership with likeminded organizations aimed at creating a new planetary civilization, we resolve to focus our energies on developing Wisdom-in-Action: a tangible, comprehensive strategic plan of action, to help ignite an emergent critical mass of awakened global citizens.

The Global Emergency Declaration
Crisis and Opportunity

There is no doubt that we are in a state of global emergency, a worldwide crisis. This crisis is a symptom of a deeper problem—the state of our consciousness: how we think about ourselves, and our world. We have the urgent need, and now also the opportunity, for a complete rethink: to reconsider our values and priorities, to understand our interconnectedness and start in a new direction, living in harmony with nature, each other, and the cosmos.

All over the world, millions of forward-thinking groups and individuals are already addressing the opportunities and not just the threats of the crisis. In every corner of the planet, designs for better systems, structures, and technologies are being developed across all fields of life. This worldwide awakening is a hopeful sign of the vitality of the human spirit and of our power to respond to the dangers we face with insight and creativity.

As yet, the sum total of our current efforts does not match the depth and urgency of the necessary transformation. But if we act together with vision, foresight, and commitment, we can lay the foundations of a global community that is both peaceful and sustainable. We can ensure our survival and wellbeing, as well as that of the next generations. As global citizens, our top planetary priority is now to create a worldwide transformation while we have the opportunity and the time to do so.

The Global Situation

If we continue on our present unsustainable path, by mid-century, the Earth could become largely uninhabitable for humanity and countless other forms of life. This global crisis affects every person, community, and society in the world through climate change, economic breakdown, ecosystem collapse, population pressure, food and water shortages, depletion of natural resources, and nuclear threats. However, a total system-collapse could occur much sooner, caused by runaway eco-catastrophes, or by escalating wars triggered by religious, geopolitical, or resource conflicts.

These threats are real. The underlying causes have been building momentum for decades, and could soon become irreversible. Estimates of when the "points of no return" will be reached have been reduced from the end of the century, to mid-century, to the next twenty years, and now to the next five to ten years.

It now appears that the "window of opportunity" for pulling out of the present crisis and breaking through to a peaceful and sustainable world may not be more than a few years from now. This timeline coincides with the many forecasts and prophecies that speak of the ending of the current cycle of human life on this planet before the end of 2012, and the dawning of a new consciousness and a new world.

An Urgent Call

We accordingly issue this urgent call to all the peoples of the world to deepen our awareness of both the dangers and the opportunities of the global crisis We hereby declare our firm commitment to work together to bring about a timely and positive WorldShift in all sectors and at all levels of society, for the survival and well-being of all the peoples of the human community and the flowering of all life on Earth.

References and Further Reading

Artigiani, Robert. "From Epistemology to Cosmology: Post-Modern Science and the Search for New Cultural Cognitive Maps," in Ervin Laszlo, Robert Artigiani, Allan Combs, and Vilmos Csányi. *Changing Visions: Human Cognitive Maps Past, Present, and Future.* Westport, CT: Praeger, 1996.

Benor, Daniel J. *Spiritual Healing: Scientific Validation of a Healing Revolution [Healing Research, Vol. 1].* Southfield, MI: Vision Publications, 2001.

———. "Survey of spiritual healing research." *Contemporary Medical Research* 4:9 (1990).

Bohm, David. *Wholeness and the Implicate Order.* Boston: Routledge & Kegan Paul, 1980.

Braud, W., and M. Schlitz. "Psychokinetic influence on electrodermal activity." *Journal of Parapsychology* 47 (1983).

Buks, E., R. Schuster, M. Heiblum, D. Mahalu, and V. Umansky. "Dephasing in electron interference by a 'which-path' detector." *Nature* 391 (February 26, 1998).

Celente, Gerald. "Global simplicity." *Trends Journal* 6:1 (Winter 1997).

Clay, Jason. *World Agriculture and the Environment.* Washington, DC: Island Press, 2004.

Crick, Francis. *The Astonishing Hypothesis: The Scientific Search for the Soul.* New York: Scribner, 1994.

Davies, Paul. *God and the New Physics.* New York: Simon & Schuster, 1983.

———. *The Mind of God.* New York: Simon & Schuster, 1992.

———, and John Gribbin. *The Matter Myth.* New York: Simon & Schuster, 1992.

Dossey, Larry. *Recovering the Soul: A Scientific and Spiritual Search.* New York: Bantam, 1989.

———. *Healing Words: The Power of Prayer and the Practice of Medicine.* San Francisco, CA: HarperSanFrancisco, 1993.

Dürr, S., T. Nonn, and G. Rempe. "Origin of quantum-mechanical complementarity probed by a 'which-way' experiment in an atom interferometer." *Nature* 395 (September 3, 1998).

Elgin, Duane, *Awakening Earth: Exploring the Evolution of Human Culture and Consciousness.* New York: Morrow, 1993.

———. *Global Consciousness Change: Indicators of an Emerging Paradigm.* San Anselmo, CA: Millennium Project, 1997.

Elkin, A. P. (Adolphus Peter). *The Australian Aborigines.* Sydney: Angus & Robertson, 1942.

Fund for Global Awakening. *In Our Own Words 2000 Research Program.* Point Reyes Station, CA: Fund for Global Awakening, 2001.

Giscard d'Estaing, Olivier. *Enterprise Ethique.* Paris: Le Cercle d'Ethique des Affaires, 1998.

Goodwin, Brian. "Development and evolution." *Journal of Theoretical Biology* 97 (1982).

———. "Organisms and minds as organic forms." *Leonardo* 22:1 (1989).

Gore, Al. *Earth in the Balance: Ecology and the Human Spirit.* Boston: Houghton Mifflin, 1992.

Grinberg-Zylverbaum, Jacobo, M. Delaflor, M. E. Sanchez-Arellano, M. A. Guevara, and M. Perez. "Human communication and the electrophysiological activity of the brain." *Subtle Energies* 3:3 (1993).

Grof, Stanislav. *The Adventure of Self-Discovery.* Albany: State University of New York Press, 1988.

———. *The Cosmic Game.* Albany: State University of New York Press, 1998.

———, with Hal Zina Bennett. *The Holotropic Mind.* San Francisco, CA: HarperSanFrancisco, 1992.

Hansen, G. M., M. Schlitz, and C. Tart. "Summary of Remote Viewing Research." In Russell Targ and K. Harary. *The Mind Race.* New York: Villard, 1984.

Haroche, Serge. "Entanglement, decoherence and the quantum/classical boundary." *Physics Today* (July 1998).

Health of the Planet: Survey. International Environment Monitor Ltd. (IEML). Ottawa, 1997.

Ho, Mae-Wan. *The Rainbow and the Worm: The Physics of Organisms.* River Edge, NJ: World Scientific, 1993.

———. "The Physics of Organisms and the Naturalistic Ethics of Wholeness." In David Lorimer, Chris Clarke, John Cosh, Max Paye, and Alan Mayne (eds). *Wider Horizons: Explorations in Science and Human Experience.* Gibliston Mill, Scotland: Scientific and Medical Network, 1999.

Honorton, C., R. Berger, M. Varvoglis, M. Quant, P. Derr, E. Schechter, and D. Ferrari. "Psi-communication in the Ganzfeld: Experiments with an automated testing system and a comparison with a meta-analysis of earlier studies." *Journal of Parapsychology* 54 (1990).

Hoyle, Fred. *The Intelligent Universe.* New York: Holt, Rinehart, and Winston, 1984.

Human Development Report 1996. United Nations Development Programme. Mahbub ul Haq and Richard Jolly, principal coordinators. New York: Oxford University Press, 1996.

Laszlo, Ervin. *The Creative Cosmos.* Edinburgh: Floris Books, 1993.

———. *The Choice: Evolution or Extinction?* New York: Tarcher/Putnam, 1994.

———. *The Interconnected Universe.* River Edge, NJ: World Scientific, 1995.

———. *Evolution: The General Theory.* Cresskill, NJ: Hampton Press, 1996.

———. *The Systems View of the World.* Cresskill, NJ: Hampton Press, 1996.

———. *The Whispering Pond.* Rockport, MA: Element Books, 1996.

———. *The Connectivity Hypothesis: Foundations of an Integral Science of Quantum, Cosmos, Life, and Consciousness.* Albany: State University of New York Press, 2001.

———. *Science and the Akashic Field: An Integral Theory of Everything.* Rochester, VT: Inner Traditions, 2004.

———. *Science and the Reenchantment of the Cosmos.* Rochester, VT: Inner Traditions, 2006.

———, Stanislav Grof, and Peter Russell. *The Consciousness Revolution: A Transatlantic Dialogue.* Boston: Element Books, 1999.

———, and Christopher Laszlo. *The Insight Edge: An Introduction to the Theory and Practice of Evolutionary Management.* Westport, CT: Quorum, 1997.

Lovelock, James, *The Revenge of Gaia.* London: Penguin, 2006.

Loye, David (ed.). *The Evolutionary Outrider: The Impact of the Human Agent on Evolution. Essays Honoring Ervin Laszlo.* Westport, CT: Praeger, 1998.

Montecucco, Nitamo. "Ricerche Olistiche." *Cyber* (Milan), November 1992.

Myers, David G. "The Social Psychology of Sustainability" in Ervin Laszlo and Peter Seidel, eds., *Global Survival: The Challenge and Its Implications for Thinking and Acting.* New York: Select Books, 2006.

Nelson, John E. *Healing the Split.* Albany: State University of New York Press, 1994.

Netherton, Morris, and Nancy Shiffrin. *Past Lives Therapy.* New York: Morrow, 1978.

Penrose, Roger. *The Emperor's New Mind.* New York: Oxford University Press, 1989.

Persinger, M. A., and S. Krippner. "Dream ESP experiments and geomagnetic activity." *Journal of the American Society for Psychical Research* 83 (1989).

Puthoff, Harold A., "Source of vacuum electromagnetic zero-point energy." *Physical Review A,* 40:9 (1989).

————, and Russell Targ. "A perceptual channel for information transfer over kilometer distances: Historical perspective and recent research." *Proceedings of the IEEE* 64 (1976).

Ray, Paul H. "American lives." *Noetics Sciences Review* (Spring 1996).

————, and Sherry Ruth Anderson. *The Cultural Creatives: How 50 Million People Are Changing the World.* New York: Harmony, 2000.

Reyner, J. H., George Laurence, and Carl Upton, revised by Keith Suter, with foreword by Ervin Laszlo. *Psionic Medicine.* Saffron Walden, Essex, UK: C. W. Daniel, 2001.

Russell, Peter. *The Global Brain Awakens: Our Next Evolutionary Leap.* Palo Alto, CA: Global Brain, 1995.

Sachs, Jeffrey. *The End of Poverty.* New York: Penguin, 2005.

Scheffer, Marten, Steve Carpenter, Jonathan A. Foley, Carl Folke, and Brian Walker. "Catastrophic shifts in ecosystems." *Nature* 413 (October 11, 2001).

Targ, Russell, and Keith Harary. *The Mind Race.* New York: Villard, 1985.

————, and Harold A. Puthoff. "Information transfer under conditions of sensory shielding." *Nature* 251 (1974).

Tarnas, Richard. *The Passion of the Western Mind.* New York: Ballantine, 1993.

Tart, Charles T. *States of Consciousness.* New York: Dutton, 1975.

Taylor, Angus. *Magpies, Monkeys, and Morals: What Philosophers Say about Animal Liberation.* Orchard Park, NY: Broadview Press, 1999.

Thoreau, Henry David. "Life without principle." Available on the Internet at: http://www.transcendentalists.com/life_without_principle.htm/

Towards a Global Ethic, Chicago: Council for a Parliament of the World's Religions, 1993.

Ullman, M., and S. Krippner. *Dream Studies and Telepathy: An Experimental Approach.* New York: Parapsychology Foundation, 1970.

Universal Declaration of Human Responsibilities. The InterAction Council, September 1, 1997. http://www.interactioncouncil.org/.

Wackernagel, M., and J. D. Yount. "The ecological footprint: An indicator of progress toward regional sustainability." *Environmental Monitoring and Assessment* 51 (1998).

Wallbank, T. Walter, and Alastair M. Taylor, *Civilization Past and Present.* Chicago: Scott Foresman and Co., 1956.

World Wildlife Fund. *Living Planet Report.* London: WWF International, New Economics Foundation, and World Conservation Monitoring Centre Gland, 1998.

About the Author

Ervin Laszlo is founder and president of the Club of Budapest, founder and director of the General Evolution Research Group, president of the Private University for Economics and Ethics of Vienna, Fellow of the World Academy of Arts and Sciences, member of the International Academy of Philosophy of Science, senator of the International Medici Academy, and editor of the international periodical *World Futures: The Journal of General Evolution*. He is the author or coauthor of 47 books translated into as many as 20 languages, and the editor of another 30 volumes including a four-volume encyclopedia.

Laszlo has a Ph.D. from the Sorbonne and is the recipient of four honorary Ph.D.s (from the United States, Canada, Finland, and Hungary). He received the Peace Prize of Japan, the Goi Award in Tokyo in 2002, and the International Mandir of Peace Prize in Assisi in 2005. He was nominated for the Nobel Peace Prize in 2004 and was renominated in 2005.

Formerly Professor of Philosophy, Systems Science, and Futures Studies in various universities in the U.S., Europe, and the Far East, Laszlo lectures worldwide. He presently lives in a 400-year-old converted farmhouse in Tuscany with his Finnish-born wife Carita. His sons Christopher and Alexander, who live with their families in the United States, follow in his footsteps, the former in the sustainability and ethical management consulting field and the latter in the academic domain where he combines evolutionary theory with evolutionary community consulting.

Index

Hampton Roads Publishing Company

. . . for the evolving human spirit

Hampton Roads Publishing Company
publishes books on a variety of subjects,
including spirrituality, health and other related topics.

For a copy of our latest trade catalog,
call 978-465-0504,
or visit our website at *www.hrpub.com.*